FOR THE LOVE OF ANIMALS

Telepathic Stories as Told by the Animals

Lorraine Vanzuylen

Karen Warren

Copyright © 2024 Lorraine Vanzuylen and Karen Warren

All rights reserved. No portion of this book may be reproduced, stored in a retrieval system, or transmitted in any form or by any means—electronic, mechanical, photocopy, recording, scanning, or other—except for brief quotations in critical reviews, articles, or groups, without written permission of the author/publisher Lorraine Vanzuylen and Karen Warren.

For more information, contact :

http://telepathicstoriesbyanimals.com

ISBN - Paperback: 9798340395566

First Edition Month: 2024

Note to the reader: The writings in this book are actual stories told to the Author in the animal's own words. Once the telepathic contact has been established, the animal is in control to tell their own stories, in their words. I do not tamper with what they want to convey in any way. These written stories, their emotions, their history, their way. Grammer and structure of the narrative by the animals may be challenging to the reader, however authenticity of the writings is of main importance.

This book of writings is a true inspirational, awakening journey, thought provoking in content. Read with enjoyment down the different paths of animals.

Handwriting typeface denotes messages from both animal and spirit.

About the Author

Communicating with animals is a cherished gift from the Creator I have been blessed with. I have never taken donations to do writings, as my path in this life has been to assist people in developing a closer walk in their relationship with animals and their Creator. I pray this book inspires all who read it.

Lorraine Vanzuylen

Introduction

All the stories in this book are written through telepathic communication between the animals and the author. Telepathic communication is the transference of thought between one mind and another without any direct physical contact. Telepathy can be achieved whether the animal is physically alive or has passed over. Once a connection is made to the animal, all thoughts and messages are communicated automatically to the written word.

Sometimes, when an animal is unable to communicate directly, other spirits may assist in the process on behalf of the animal. These spirits or souls usually have a connection to the communicator or may work with animals on the Other Side. They may be animal or human entities that have finished their life cycle on Earth and reside in the heavenly realm.

Animals are a gift from God to humanity to assist with each individual's soul growth. Unconditional love, forgiveness, and trust are all common traits that our pets are born with.

Just like people, animals can incur traumatic events that

can cause them to distrust and become fearful. Uncommon behaviour and personality changes can be influenced by a negative or frightening experience encountered in the current life cycle or past incarnations. Like humans, animals incarnate to grow in soul, learn and overcome. Through communication, we can understand that there is no bad animal, only an animal that needs love and empathy.

This book is to help people have a clearer understanding of how animals think and feel and how these factors influence their behaviour. Their feelings and emotional needs are very similar to ours. They crave a sense of belonging, to love and be loved by their humans. My hope is that these writings resonate with each and every reader and that a greater understanding of the relationship between humans and animals will be achieved.

All the writings are uninhibited, direct communication. As a result, grammar or sentence structure has not been modified to ensure the writings are as genuine as possible.

Some names have been changed, and others are on a first-letter basis to protect the privacy of individuals. Enjoy!

Dedication

This book is dedicated with great joy and endless thanks to all who participated in making it happen. Especially appreciated was the willingness and patience of the animals, who so eagerly provided their opinions and perceptions, as expressed in the writings they shared. Thank you also to my three daughters for their unwavering support and belief in me and my vision for this endeavour.

I offer special gratitude to Karen for her diligent efforts in the production of this book.

Contents

About the Author ii

Introduction iii

Dedication v

Chapter One 2

    My Story 2
    Animal Relationships to Humans 6
    Life Cycles and Reincarnations 10

Chapter Two   For the Love of Dogs 12

    Hope Nash Sammy – Time to Go 12
    Trinity Franky Maizee – A Family in Turmoil 37
    Cooper – A Short Story 77
    Myah – Here, Then, There 81
    Stewie – Final Message of Love 84
    Baily – Why I Am the Way I Am 88
    Firolais – The Shelter Pup 93
    Maddie – A New Life 99
    Stella and Corona – Messages of Truth 105

Cedar – Happy Dog, Happy Life 119

Sadie's Walk of Shame 122

Gurdie – A Message of Love 127

Ellie May – 911 130

Zack and Ivan, Then Mexie.. 135

Faith – A Jealous Dog 152

Karma-Third Time's a Charm 156

Poppy, Kona and Moseley.. 165

Trixie – Not a Loss, Only a Gain.. 175

Eloise – I Choose You.. 180

Baron – Let's Talk 186

Chapter Three For the Love of Cats........................190

Chubby – From Past to Present... 190

Frieda – A Word to All... 195

Fee – The Fun-Loving Cat 201

Carmel – Choice of Return... 204

Vanilla – A Transition of Love... 209

Chapter Four For the Love of Horses 212

A Foal Born Terrified... 212

Flynn – Cause and Effect 216

Dena and Liberty – Disruption on the Farm............................... 219

Diva – Past, Present, Future	248
Belle – The Horse with an Attitude	252
Bree and Donkey	256
Stella, Chance and an Angel	258
Oliver – OOPS, Let Me Stay	264
Tilley – Big Attitude, Tiny Horse	271
Abby – Gone but Forever Present	276
Rules – A Champion Inside and Out	279
Cherokee – Happy Trails till We Meet Again	283
Moonie – His Memory Lives On	290
Gimble – It's a Wonderful Life	297
Nella – A Word from the Wise	301
Molson – Simple Lives	304
Paige – Things That Go Yelp in the Night	307
Zeta Sunni – Double the Love	312
Hitch – A Hero of His Own Story	326
Georgia – A Word of Advice	329
Reggie – A Transformation	333
Shanna, Mishka, Patti – A Story of Three	338
Tyson – A Rodeo Horse's Story	350
Ebony - An Auction Horse	357
Poco and Clair, Together Forever	371

Fanci – Misunderstanding, Regret 374
Dodo Daisy – A Cow's Story 378
AUTHORS BIOGRAPHIES **382**

Chapter One

My Story

My mother was a single mother at twenty-seven, left deserted trying to bring up her little three-year-old daughter. She scrubbed and washed floors, laundered, and did anything to survive. I was loved and secure, and I never realized the sacrifices she had made for me.

I sustained a serious injury when I was three years of age. While playing, I accidentally put my hand through the ringers of a washing machine and crushed my hand. A year of surgeries, blood poisoning, and scarlet fever left me with little hope of survival. My mother explained to me how fortunate I was. I was to lose my arm first, up to my elbow, but ended up only losing my thumb.

I relate this to you for a particular reason.

One day, my mother brought home a canary in a battered cage. He was to look after me while she worked. This bird instilled in me a positive will to live. We both sat in the sunshine that came through the window. I healed as he sang from morning to night, with no care, relying on me to look after his needs. Together, we sang songs my mother taught me as my strength returned.

My path was never clear to me. I have always doodled. I have always written but never seriously, not thinking about or believing in the source. I could not accept I had a unique Gift, and I constantly questioned it. Symbols have been with me since I learned to write with my left hand. To identify the source of the writing I always request a symbol. Different entities whether human or animal, are defined and validated through their own unique symbol.

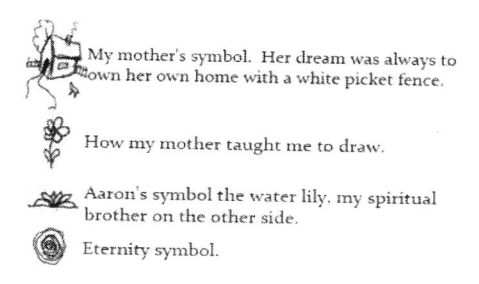

My mother's symbol. Her dream was always to own her own home with a white picket fence.

How my mother taught me to draw.

Aaron's symbol the water lily, my spiritual brother on the other side.

Eternity symbol.

Writings became intense; the subjects, unknown to me, would develop on paper. Requests came to me from family and friends, then through them, from people I did not know. There was no direct involvement. Never, ever was there any kind of reimbursement, the source of the writing unknown to them.

I started writing for animals when my daughter phoned and asked if I would do a writing for her sick horse. This seemed an impossible request, and I explained to her as much. Tears weakened me, and a surprise came forth. Pleased that I had the ability, then upset as it was written, signed "Your Hairy Horse." I was devastated. How could this be? My heart was heavy, but I proceeded to read the message to her. I tried to make excuses, then finally told her how it was signed.

My daughter said, "What's your problem, Mom? He was the hairiest horse going. He had to be shaved two to three times in the summer."

Since that writing, I have included animals in my writings with no regrets. It is sheer enjoyment to understand their abundance of love, forgiveness, sad and happy times, and their ability to easily remember prior lives, mistakes they made, lessons they learned and lives they still want to experience. They have so much to give, asking only to be respected and loved in return.

Animal Relationships to Humans

The following is a message from the Other Side explaining the truth about animals and how it pertains to their relationship with humans as meant by our Creator.

<u>Message from Spirit</u>

I wish to write about the wonderful souls of animals that God created to love and be loved: some companions, some to be for food. All have a purpose to humans, all with simple, pure souls. All animals have their own domain, self-sacrificing, so forgiving, asking only respect, understanding and kindness for complete obedience. This is true, especially for pets. Mistreating any animal is not accepted by our Creator. All animals must be appreciated, respected for their purpose in a life cycle.

Take cows, for instance. They willingly give their life to supply food for humans. This is their path in life. When treated kindly and fed properly, then they supply—abundantly—what they have to give, in abundance. To suffer unnecessarily is against the law of our Creator.

When it is time to pass over, it should be with dignity, a job well done, regardless of what capacity they serve. There is no fear to return home; it is just accepted by them. This is their time. This does not mean that they do not encounter deep sadness, leaving persons who have shown them love, whom they also loved.

Animals, like humans, are not meant to be perfect, but all should strive to be the best they can be without sorrow but in joy when facing their Creator. Animals that pass over that have been mistreated, brutally beaten, starved, many situations that cause changes to their normal behaviour will have tendencies in retaliation. What you could call handlers are on this Other Side to greet them. These souls may be ones who have mistreated animals, now wishing to make amends for their terrible actions. Their willing duties are to gain trust, show love, and work with this suffering animal for rehabilitation. This is not an easy task; many methods may be required.

Sometimes, a mistreated child can gain the trust due to a common area of understanding, sympathy for each other. An example is dogs. If they have been groomed to be guard dogs/fighting animals, their existence on Earth is difficult to erase; they have lost their purpose. Handlers who now work with them must bring out the goodness, love, and trust so that they return to their happy nature. When this has been completed, they are allowed to return for another life cycle.

This is a difficult time, as old meanness can surface. They are not bad animals; they have been mistreated animals. This is true of all the animal kingdoms. Horses, dogs, and cats attune themselves the closest to humans. They have, can develop a friendship, love, respect if treated right.

All animals are loved by their Creator

known in abundance by their souls within. Some just communicate with their actions, their eyes, see the love there as it is meant to be. This is a confusion not of words only, communicating in the animal way, deep conviction, total trust, always forgiving, to love and be loved. This is their nature, natural in abundance, not always perfect, especially in the baby stage.

This barking, gleeful time, full of mischief and happiness, has no bounds as it is another chance to prove their need to exist for humans—their unbounded love. Only animals have the ability to reach the depths of a soul, lonely, sick, in need, many ways, not through light words but with empathy, a natural ability God has given, accepted so. More will be written.

Praise the Creator, His Blessing upon all.

Life Cycles and Reincarnations

An animal's nature is true, its heart pure. They know they were created like this. Forgiveness and love abound in them naturally. They know when their time is near, accepting this life cycle. Birth, life, death.

All of creation lives more than one life. Animals are receptive; they just know and accept this will happen. Some religions call it "The Wheel of Life." Others call it the "Circle of Life" or "Life without End." Animals are more sensitive and have the ability to remember past lives naturally. If an animal has had a prior life of being mistreated or abused, it may take several lifetimes of positive human interaction for them to be restored to their natural state of love and trust.

Many of the animals in this book recall their past life cycles. Their current life may entail habits, fears, and insecurities from a former life, which they may need to overcome in this life. An understanding that this is an actual occurrence with many animals leads to a closer relationship between animals and their humans. With love, patience and compassion, the animal can prevail over these obstacles.

Chapter Two
For the Love of Dogs

Hope Nash Sammy – Time to Go

Hope was a Blue Heeler, right from the beginning a special pup. Always anxious to please, her whole life revolved around her family. One morning playing outside with the other dogs, Hope was nowhere to be found. Hope always came when called, it was apparent that something was terribly wrong. A light sheet of ice was on the water, a hole at the end of the dock showed where her tracks had abruptly stopped. The family feared the inevitable. It appeared that Hope had fallen into the river. Hours of searching turned up nothing.

A message from spirit revealed that this was truly an accident. Hope had been playing with her favorite toy. When it dropped into the river she tried to retrieve it and fell into the icy water. A writing from the other side explained Hope was drifting in and out between dimensions. She fought to stay with her family but eventually succumbed, passing in the arms of strangers, the ones who had tried to save her. Once on the other side, Hope connected with a departed family member. When Hope passed the mutual love for the family acted as a magnetic, immediately bonding these two souls.

Once Hope had undergone healing, she was ready to communicate. She conveyed her love for her family and what she was doing on the other side.

Hope's remains were never found despite days of searching. Her toy was eventually discovered down river.

Message from Spirit Looking for Hope

Owner's QUESTION: Hope, the pup is missing. What happened?

Spirit's REPLY: *We are watching for her, and she does not appear to have come home (Other Side) yet. We try to locate her, but I can't find her down there. Hope may be the right name as she may be in a different dimension, which could be why we cannot find her.*

There… is now clear she has joined us and is home

safe. It was an accident; wanted to play, slipped, and water too cold. Not sure what happened. Don't tell the owner yet, as still passing back and forth. It was before her time. We will watch over her, but not our decision to make. Do not worry; loved on both sides.

We see her now. She has been rescued. Good people have found her, wrapped in a blanket, trying to revive her. Still fighting to survive to return to you. She's looked after either way. If she returns home, I will take her with me. You may not see her again, but know she will be in good hands. I will let you know.

Tell the owners that Hope is here with me, safe in my arms. She chose me (Henk) to be my companion. This was like a Christmas gift, a wonderful token, so loving, from them both. Sad for your loss, but an unexpected gift, so precious. She will need time to heal as it was a sudden and true accident. I don't know exactly how we—I guess you would say bonded— it was a mutual love we both had for them. She will heal, and we will be together always, underfoot, and joy as my Christmas gift. Find peace and maybe know Jesus loves and takes care of all types of his flock.

<u>First Message from Hope After Passing</u>

Maw has asked if you could write from me. Hope was a name that made me feel special. I do not know of any pet that has been named Hope. I had a special name for you, not like any others had. I enjoyed naming you Maw and Paw. It made you both special to me. I know I was not able to be obedient, but I did try. I couldn't let Paw sleep as there was too much fun to be had. I needed to know everything; I had to be exploring every minute. Don't look for me, but know this is my heaven, secure and loved as when I was with you. Remember me with love as I remember you. God created me with love, and this I send to you, my Maw and Paw.

Second Message from Hope and Her Duties on the Other Side

This is Hope. Maw and Paw, I was only with you for a short, hectic time. You named me Hope, and I want you to know why. Our Creator does not make mistakes. I now know why I was your doggie and the reason why I was named Hope. I am and always will be just that: a reminder of hope.

Your illness, Paw, when upset, I was near you to give you hope for the future. This is thought-provoking. Henk, my pal, told me to say this as it is a mix-up all to do with hope. I hope I will make you, Maw and Paw, smile, as we are bound in friendship and love. I opened the door to your hearts as you did mine. Henk and I do everything together, by each other's side, bound by a mutual love for you still on Earth.

You may wonder what we do, always side by side. It is like we are to look after a lost soul, confused, maybe passed over in bad faith or accident like me. Not all was able to have someone on this side watch for them like Henk and me. Together, we work to help that soul. Love, patience, kindness, then the belief they are loved. No soul is lost to our Creator. I am not so good with patience. Henk is now. But love, I have lots of. This you taught me. I am your Hope in so many different ways.

Believe so. God's Light shines upon you. Bones are pretty good here.

Hope/Henk

Third Message from Hope

I wish to tell Jay my Paw, that I am near him always. Henk understands we are close, but you are my special one. Each human has much more to deal with, always emotions, feelings, and temptation. Animals are all pure of heart. This is how our Creator made all. All have special paths to follow; mine is with you. When you have pain reach out to me as I am always near you, unconditional love and concern. I love Maw, but you are special. Many lives together, all rewarding.

You saved me from terrible situations, always there for me, healing and caring. My wish has been granted that always be here to console you also. I suffer your pain and frustration. I understand what is on your mind. I am sensitive as if we were one as we have been together through many situations; that is our bond everlasting. There are many souls here, not all known to you in this life, sending many our Creator's Blessings. Know I am by your side, knowing your pain and frustration. Reach out to me. I am always with you, almost like a Guardian Angel, doggy kind.

Maw named me Hope. I give you Creator's Blessing, Love and Hope, my dearest Maw and Paw.

NASH'S STORY

Nash a Black Lab Cross who was also part of the same family as Hope. Nash had been adopted into the family when he was surrendered to the Humane Society as a year-old pup.

The first time Nash met his owner, he knocked her to the ground and bit her in excitement. At that moment she knew she could not leave without that dog.

From the beginning Nash was a going concern. Playful with never-ending energy. His owners had to be attentive to where he was and what he was getting into. If it was not screwed down it was fair game for Nash. Shoes, shirts, everything was free for the taking. Nash was a very kind, sociable dog. Every animal that was introduced into the household was Nash's immediate buddy. Time passed; Nash began to slow down. Nash developed a lump on his leg when he was 11 years old. Diagnosed as cancer, it had spread through the rest of his body. Nash writes about his love for his family, not wanting to leave but knowing his time was near. His supportive words reassuring his family he would always remain close. His last message was conveyed through the aid of Hope and the departed family member. Nash left this world about 3 months after his initial diagnosis.

First Message from Nash When Diagnosed with Cancer

You have asked for my inner feelings, which are confusing to me. Mixed up. I have never lived a life such as with you. I know who you are. My friends and I am so happy with you. Do not ask me if I want to pass on, as I would answer NO. Life, loved as we are, cannot want to go out. When my time comes, I will have to, but not what is here now for me. I hold on for every moment, wishing there was more time for me. Dogs have true love; most humans don't, but you both do.

<u>Near-End Message from Nash</u>

This is your pet called Nash. When I look into your eyes, my mistress, I see all your care, concern and love. You don't like to see me suffer as I am. My thoughts are getting all over that it makes me sad not to remember other days, fun days which are not there for me now. I am at peace. I know my time is near. Do you not know I see you in anguish when you look at me? You both suffer with me. I would like to tell you to suffer no more over me as I am prepared; it is my time. However it happens, I wish you to remember me the way I was—always. I will never leave, as my spirit will always be with you both. Know, just drop your hand down, and I am there, ready to be by your side. I am the most happy loving dog to have known this lifestyle with you both and my friends.

<u>Nash's Final Message</u>

I feel, but I can't remember all I wish to take with me when I return home. I will have all my memories returned to me then. Now, I am in the passing time, neither here nor there. I lay here quietly, waiting till I am called. Soon, it will happen, which way I do not mind. Someone from home is with me. He wants you to know I will always be beside him, companion until you are with me on this side. He tells me his name, but I am too weak to be able to hear properly. He has a tender touch, not like you, but there.

He draws me ever closer with him, trying to ease my pain. I will meet more friends, Hope (his companion who passed previously) and I will have fun together. His name sounds like He, but I am too weak to know. I wish to say that you, we all call Ma and Pa, with love bursting from our hearts. I am ready to go home, and I am sick and weak. Hope and He are adding strength so I can finish my words. I am tired. I can take all my memories with me and will visit often. I will still take most of the bed when I sleep with you; bad habit, but oh, so nice.

Tired, but giving all my love,

Nash

SAMMY'S STORY

Sammy was a fun-loving lab cross acquired at four months of age by his family. As a pup, she always seemed to be getting into mischief, but as she matured, she became a trustworthy companion. Sammy developed hip dysplasia at a young age, which was controlled through herbal medicine. Sammy communicates her love for her family then talks about her previous life as a guardian dog. As time passed, Sammy started experiencing severe issues with movement and sleep disruption. X-ray's revealed Sammy had cancer. Her condition continued to deteriorate at a rapid rate. Her last message was communicated through Nash, her lifelong friend who had passed years earlier. She was put to rest shortly after her last message, her family by her side. She was thirteen years of age.

First Message from Sammy

Sammy, for my loved ones. When they say pets, it means so much more than just that word. Love, kindness when I was not the best pet. I challenged you so many different ways to see if you still loved me. You always did. I am sorry, I still cuddle up in bed with you. You know, don't you? I am a happy Sammy where I am, but I wonder why you never named another pet with my name. I wasn't that bad, was I? I showed you both my love unconditionally, whether I was good or bad. I will always be your pet, Sammy.

Till we are together, it's going to be a bit crowded as you sure are accumulating pets. The Creator made us all so that we can be together.

Till then,

Sammy

Second Message from Sammy Recalling a Past Life

You ask questions of me, Sammy, which makes me happy. I am close to Nash, and we are close. I feel a loss for this one called Nash; we were close. I feel my time draws near. I don't know if I am sick or depressed. I wish to be neither, but I don't know. Nash tells me wonderful stories of the Other Side, but I do not want to leave. The Other Side could not be anything like the comforts of home, so nice, so loving. Why would I want to leave? I won't be upset anymore.

If I am sick, then that is because I don't know. In my prior life, I was on a farm. Times, they say, were tough, but I was well looked after. My job was to look after keeping the chickens and other animals safe. I was big and ferocious when needed to be but gentle with the children. I took my duties seriously and never ever let anything bad happen.

I fought with a wolf; I was bigger, but he was more vicious. I saved the livestock but had serious injuries, which I don't know, but I was never the same. I wasn't able to do my duties as the attack had weakened me. They still loved me and looked after me till I passed. The injuries made me suffer great pain; the children looked after me so gently, so loving, never angry, but just so careful.

Towards the end, my master carried me, telling me it was a job well done. He cried when I passed, thanking me for saving his children, baby and two others. I had tears in my eyes as he did, too. I willingly would have given my life many times over to protect them. It was not only my duty but my thanks to the Creator to give me the strength to protect them. I have an easy life now, Miss Nash, but not ready to go. I write this so you know my happiness and gratitude to be your dog, Sammy.

QUESTION: I don't understand. You say livestock and children.

Sammy's REPLY: *Yes, I will tell you. There was hunger in the woods. I fought furiously when attacked by a wolf. I knew he was stalking the animals, so I pretended to be asleep. He kept circling closer and closer. I lunged at him; we fought, many injuries. He finally sulked away. I was slowly healing. I was to protect the children outside playing. The two older ones were to look after the baby. I was attacked by a wolf who was after the children. I fought with all the strength I had. Man heard the screaming, grabbed his rifle and shot the wolf. I could not move. They carried me on a rug inside* the house. I was never allowed inside the house, only outside.

I lay unable to move. The gentle pats of the children trying to feed me, singing to me, many tears from my eyes and theirs. Finally, with the children kneeling and praying for me to get better, I passed over. A grave was dug, and the children made a cross, loving prayers said. The two older children could not agree on my name, so I was called Big Mike. I answered to both. So now you know why I like the bed.

Our Creator loves Sammy.

Third Message from Sammy as Her Sickness Progresses

I saw my friend Nash and others I have been with before. I feel different like I don't remember before. I can't help you because I don't know what's wrong. My legs feel weak, and my body just doesn't want to be me. I am not scared, but just don't know what is wrong. Nash says the Creator will look after me and know when it is my time to pass over. It feels like this, but I do not want to leave. Maybe some medicine could help me. I want to feel better, but Nash says it is not my decision. I don't want to leave my family here, even to be with Nash and the others. If nothing can be done, then I accept. But try medicine for me. Maybe someone will know what is happening to me as I don't know.

My complete life and happiness have been right here. I have seen and experienced the passing over of so many of my companions and always have felt the loss, but they always tell me the same thing. When it is your time, you must go. Sometimes, the strong love we experience with the family and companions holds us longer, but time happens, time to go. Try medicine. I don't want to go, but not well, need help; my body sick, ache to move.

Always love for my family and Nash.

Message from Nash on Behalf of Sammy

This is Nash. You gave me such loving care that will never be forgotten. I write as Sammy is in great pain. She is unable to write—doesn't want you both to know. She wishes to stay with you as long as she can, but the pain is becoming unbearable for her. She asks, could she remain home with something to take the pain away? She knows it is her time; not afraid to come home, but every moment she can stay means a lot to her. Memories till the last moment of her family. She wishes her last moments to be looking at her family. She cannot bear the pain and wishes to be free of it. Stay with her until she passes. Rub her neck as before, patting her. This would be a beautiful passing for her. How this happens is alright with her as she knows this side has many friends to see.

The other dog in the house is sad not only for Sammy but knows that her parting will be difficult. She knows the care and love she has *lived in, she also will have the same anguish in parting from her family. This is the cycle for all, our Creator's way of our gaining many lessons to know as we grow in heart and soul as with Sammy, a loving companion.*

Nash for Sammy

During communication with Nash, Nash facilitated interaction between Lorraine and an 'Unknown Spirit Dog'. This dog that had endured deplorable abuse during his/her life cycle on Earth wished to explain Nash's roll in his healing on the other side. This is a testimony of what happens to a soul once they transition to the Other Side and have experienced such horrific circumstances. Whether it be human or animal, all souls undergo a process of healing and rehabilitation after their life on earth.

Message from the Long-Lost Dog
==============================

This is only a long-lost animal left out in the cold to die. I see all the happy animals with happy homes, not that I am not happy on this side, but would have wished for a better life cycle. There are rewards for suffering, a higher vibration that brings you closer to your Creator. My connection to you is my friend Nash. I enjoy the many memories of the cycle of life spent with the family, loved by all.

Nash and I are buddies, bonded. We offset each other as I had such terrible Earth memories, and Nash had such a good life; works with me to change my memories for the better. Once I am healed, I will be able to help others to overcome what happened in their life cycle. Change viciousness to gentle, especially those used as guard dogs, fighting rings, abused or neglected like I was. Dogs like Nash reach the ones like us, easing our terrible prior existence, bringing memories of prior good lives.

I am healing under Nash's kind love, which is why I am writing to you. I thought you would be pleased to know. Our existence in life cycles on Earth is to be companions to humans. In return for our loyalty, we hope for kindness, respect—most of all, love. Nash had all this and more. I am learning from Nash to be so. I don't have a name from this prior life, only "Stupid Dog." Thank you for Nash. We send our Creator's Blessing.

Later Communication with the "Stupid Dog"

STATEMENT TO DOG: Nash's owner wants you to be named Precious. Her heart goes out to you, and she would like to give you a big hug.

Unknown Dog REPLY: *Nash told me about you. How he always slept with you, too, sometimes selfishly taking your part of the bed. Your heart is full, enough for all but still enough to love me, sight unseen. I can only heal with so much abundance of love. Nash told me, but I could not imagine. Now I know "stupid dog" now becomes Precious under the love sent to me. From my friend Nash, I was told love heals, but now I believe this to be true.*

Trinity Franky Maizee – A Family in Turmoil

Trinity was adopted into the family when the owners were having problems with predators killing their chickens. From the word GO, Trinity was a holy terror. A puppy so curious that she wanted to experience and do everything her own way. Conveyed in the writing as a magnificent animal that did not answer to anyone or anything but to herself ONLY. Problems occurred. Trinity started killing chickens and had unpredictable, threatening behavior towards her owners and the other animals on the farm. She wandered wherever she wanted, getting into trouble and going places she was not to go. All efforts to train Trinity were in vain. As a last-ditch effort, telepathic communications were invoked to try to resolve these issues.

In the first writing Trinity explains that her uncontrollable behavior had been carried over from her previous life cycle into this life. Her love for her family was strong, but not as strong as her predatorial instincts. She was concerned as to whether she could change, and feared her aggressive behavior would escalate.

She then further explained her past life, her need to kill and her need for revenge.

Trinity's First Message

This is Trinity, who came to you knowing of your care and love abundant. If anyone could help me, it would be you. I chose to be a small animal in order to control myself and to do as little harm as possible to others. I wish to explain.

My prior life was as a powerful predator, a king of the jungle. There was nothing that was not my prey. This life and a prior, I was not to, should not have to kill for food. The instinct within me still so strong that I don't know how to control the urge to kill. A prey is not needed as food is plentiful.

You cannot always watch me, as I will as soon as loose, bound for some kind of prey. This has been the best I have ever been, but not good enough. Mumba (Mom): it is like your smoking; it cannot be controlled. The difference is you only hurt yourself; I hurt others, picking on defenceless animals. Shame is mine. I don't know how I can change as love and food abundant is not enough for my instinct to kill and taste blood.

Your kind heart and J's know what you should do. You have given me chances to change, but I know not how. I can't undo what is part of me. My fear is it may just keep getting worse. I need more of our Creator's healing. Even the whip, my symbol, cannot take it out of me.

The Creator be with you, understand.

A Few Hours Later: Message from Trinity Distrusting Herself

Trinity just wants you to know I need our Creator's healing Grace. When I am strong again, I will try to come to you in joy and healed. This is not as you think, as humans, a sin. I just need more time to heal instincts too strong to handle now. This also happens with humans, and our Creator takes us into His loving care to be healed and restored as He created us so lovingly to be so. I know you are determined to change me, but I believe it will only cause more hurt. I do not want this to be so, as I love this family.

Message from Trinity Recalling Her Past Life

Trinity, wishing to tell you why I must

overcome what I am and why. I obeyed our Creator's law, killing only what is needed to live. Respect all humans and animals. Many lives this was so. Then, I became a different creature. Big, huge, beautiful. I could roar to scare others but showed off only, never ever did anything against our Creator's law. Maybe this was the goodness of living. I had peace and was happy. I became brave and powerful, wandering out of the jungle. Men saw me and wanted me as a trophy. They wanted the honour of being the one to kill me, not for hunger, no law of ours, only this trophy that they had killed. I was hurt, shot with bullets that stung my body and made me bleed.

I survived after a long time of hurting. I almost starved as I was unable to hunt for food. Revenge was all I thought about. This kept me alive. When strength was regained, I became powerful enough to seek out humans, men, anything that stood in my way. I wandered farther out of my domain to kill the ones that had caused me so much pain, nearly starving to death. I was injured and shot many more times, which I survived, and made me more brutal, needed to revenge more. Packs of men came out together to kill me as I was completely out of control. Nothing but revenge each time I was hurt; there was nothing to stop one killing all in my way. Finally, my Creator called me home.

There are stories told of me when they see my head on a plaque, arguing over the price it is worth still. God, your God, my Creator, surrounded me with love. All animals I had killed in lust forgave me. I was finding peace within. Finally, I wanted to try another life again. It felt good inside that I could overcome my past, make up into a loving pet, and be obedient, the opposite to what I was. I tried and cannot be what I want to be. I need what only my Creator can do for me. We tried to put all the protection not to let my history repeat itself. I know I am doing wrong, and I know how disobedient I am. I am just repeating my history on a smaller scale. I have this written so I can also tell you about my love for this family I am part of.

You are patient, even still caring for me after destroying your animals, which you lovingly care for. I know the hurt I am causing. If anyone could have changed me, it would be you. You know now my story, the horrors I went through and the terrible horrors I revenged on others. Even though it is not true in this life, it still comes through. You and the family have done all you can do. Now you do understand, always.

Trinity

FRANKY'S STORY

Franky was adopted into the family when her previous owner became terminally sick and could not care for the dog. The adjustment was difficult. Franky was nervous all the time and the owners could not decipher what her issues were. As it turned out Trinity would not accept Franky. Much of Trinity's predatorial and aggressive behavior was still lingering from her past life. Franky tried to make peace, but Trinity's hostile behavior continued. Trinity was trying, but somehow could not overcome her past. Then the accident.

Message from Franky

My collar is worn with pride. I am a dog that just wants to be loved, obey and please. I am scared all the time. Don't know what to do. Just want what I knew before to be the same, but don't know how it can be. I want happiness and to be one of the group, as there is love all around enough for all.

Trinity longs for what I am like, but her nature is not so. Her anger within scares me. Even if she killed me, it would not make any difference to her, not even satisfaction. When I tried to guide her and explain, she becomes angry and is mean to me. I tried to make myself small and not seen, but she still seeks me out for vengeance. What do I do? Where do I hide? I know love is there for us all, harmony, fun but this doesn't work due to her nature. She wants control but doesn't know how to control herself. She is herself own worst enemy. She has a loving nature, but so deep down. She won't let it be. Sad I am to say these words, but I am unable to help her as she will not accept the example of her animal friends. We could be so content and happy but realize that we all want to save her from herself.

Sometimes, we have fun, but she forgets who she is now in this life. This happens. I know some prior instincts stronger than others we come back with. Remind her this is her last chance in this life cycle, and we all will try to. We know and love our family and understand the sacrifices our parents make; this does not go without here and above. Know not all is lost guidance from above. I am in the right place to help try to be stronger. Our Maker's Blessing. Franky

Trinity had been wandering around on a public lane when the neighbors trail camera took her picture. A threatening message was delivered to the owners that the dog would be eliminated if found near the property again. Despite the owner's efforts of building fences, putting up gates, Trinity could not be contained. Trinity explains on the day of the accident she was wandering around the neighbor's property. The neighbor threatened her, and she retaliated. He disposed of her and left her for dead, but somehow Trinity managed to make it home.

After disappearing for hours Trinity was discovered, covered in mud laying on the corner of the lawn. Unable to walk she had somehow dragged herself home. For days she laid still, unable to eat or drink, uncontrollable urination of blood, it was thought she wouldn't make it. Finally, Trinity started to gain back her strength, it looked like she would survive. Trinity was given one last chance to redeem herself. She recalls asking for an opportunity to change her ways. She was left with a limp as a reminder that if she did not change, she would be called back home (other side).

Message from Trinity on the Road to Recovery

This is Trinity, your dog, so set in her ways that obedience was not for her. Even love could not bind me to listen as I had always been the absolute only. My Creator and the others on the Other Side had problems controlling me. I was the roaring, almighty animal refusing to be tamed in any way by anyone, even from my Creator. This history is what I was to change; be docile and obedient. This was my opportunity to make amends and change. If anyone could help and guide me, it was the special human I love.

He has tried to protect me against myself, those animal instincts so bred in me for the survival I needed for the other life. I have been reminded what I was to achieve in this life. I should have passed over, but it was the tears and prayers of the one that always forgave me.

    I promised my Creator if I was permitted to live, just one more chance to be what I wanted to be, not for myself but the one who is caring so diligently to save me. I understand I will live, but they, my Creator, has left me a cripple, within and without, as a reminder of what my goal was to be to redeem myself from prior lives. I could never find anyone so patient, loving of another family that would be there to support and forgive me for my willful ways. The saving tears, prayer and love all for me unselfishly. Praise our Creator for his forgiving love. Trinity is the right name.

Message from Trinity Further Explaining Her Past Life and Given a Last Chance to Redeem Herself After the Accident

Trinity, again, as must explain my wrong way. Created I was to protect all around me. Magnificent, strong, no one could challenge me. As time went on, I could see fear in eyes. This made me different than what was intended. Fear, I enjoyed. I could roar and all around, scurried out of my way. No one could make me do anything different. I was the Only, no Creator, only I. Humans, I said, wanted me as a trophy. What they did to me rendered me weak; this I could not accept. Dying, weakening each day. My mate who was with me was of no meaning but, for instinct, feared me. She felt I was dying, weak, left quietly in the night. I was alone, no food, unable to hunt for myself. Revenge kept me going. There was and never could be anything or anyone as powerful as me, Only. I did just what I wanted to do. Here was no pity, no love, nothing but Only. I won't repeat this part again as this is not what I want to tell you.

I went home, as was the cycle. Difficulties arose when I saw that I had become vindictive and mean, stronger. Eventually, those on the Other Side worked hard to make me understand that this was not why I was created. Great strides were accomplished, so I wished to make amends. I had not known love, kindness, so a special family was chosen, love for all animals, and others like me being cherished. This was the plan to change me and not fall into the wrong ways.

I learned to live with others, humans and animals. I have tried so many times to be obedient as my other companions. Know this as true. I still have difficulty being controlled. I don't think; I just do. I have improved. So much to overcome, but so much is still within.

I never knew love or respect, but it has happened for the someone special to me. The one that always forgives me, the only one that I accept as my master. I was becoming out of control again, so my Creator called me home. Even after I wanted another chance, I lost my way. I have never asked for forgiveness, ever in my creation, but I ask now from my Creator and you. I am slowly regaining what my purpose in life should be. If I become out of control again then no more chances. I will be called home.

I was not completely without a mechanism to remind me when I turned to old ways—a reminder in pain is there. Few would have put up with me. My lessons are being learned, but know that your efforts to help me overcome what I was is appreciated, not only here but on the Other Side. You were my last hope. I will try harder, but it is not a lack of love for my family or true love for my master, but the terrible strong instinct left over from another life. My future is mine; how I overcome it.

Trinity

Sixth Message Remembering the Accident

Trinity. I remember now and wish to tell you. I was prowling around as I like to do. The man caught me on his domain and attacked me. I retaliated instead of running away. I am told this was wrong, but I thought I had to protect myself. He started beating me with some wooden plank. I lunged at the man, and he hit me hard, trying to kill me. I am not sure what happened next. I came to, and man was carrying me. I was heavy for him but could not do anything; so sick, I think. It was dark, and man was stumbling. We came to water. The man tried to throw me in but couldn't do it. I fell on the edge of the water but not in. I know man tried to drown me, couldn't, so left me to die. If this were to happen, then I wanted to be with my family, those who showed me love and patience.

I must decide now if I can change myself for an obedient one, change the instincts from a prior life. I realize how powerful strong I was but *should not have used it to retaliate against humans, who succeeded in killing me. Revenge was too strong, and my ending. I was to reverse this in this life, make up for amends, become obedient, finding and giving love. I must think now, if I can do this, my decision that only I can make. My friends—the other animals—are trying to help me, as are my loved ones, so precious.*

Hold strong for me.   Trinity

After the accident Trinity's demeanor began to change. No longer was she a threat to the chickens. She accepted the other dogs as family; she was now the protector not the predator. Her aggressive behavior had diminished. She watched over the property and never wandered, always staying close to the house. She displayed affection openly to her owners and became obedient, loving and respectful. Her message was one of pride as her new role as protector.

Another Message from Trinity to Her Family, One Year Later

Look at me, happy and at peace. I have found myself, love, kind to others, all there to experience for me. Truly not perfect, but so at peace within. I protect my family; I will not let anyone near unless they are a friend. I will try to not allow any danger. I try to do this as my love for this family has overcome so much I did wrong. Obedient, I am working on, but I am their protector as this is what I want to be. My family has shown me the way to our Creation, how we are to be, my purpose fulfilling peace for me, love for my forgiving family.

My Creator has shown me the way. I am not a guard dog, predator, but a protector of my family. Mumba, you know this.

Trinity

Shortly after this message, Trinity was found standing over a dead chicken. Later that day, another chicken was found dead in a location that Trinity was unable to access. The owner requested a writing to determine if she had digressed into her old ways and had killed the chicken or if the dead chickens died from other causes.

<u>Message from Trinity</u>

Owner's QUESTION: Did you kill the chicken?

Trinity's REPLY: *I am Trinity. You punished me, and I don't know why. I brought the chicken out of the henhouse to see what happened. Before, if I wanted prey, I would stalk them, ravish them for the excitement. I do not do this. You know how I used to be so horrible, torture for the fun. You know this bird was not mauled, no blood. I know I don't deserve to be trusted, but I am not like that no more. I feel sad inside. I should have left the bird inside. I will prove to you I am worthy of love and trust. I was curious why that bird didn't move. I took it outside to see why. I knew I had not done anything to it, so why did it not move? I said I was not a guard dog. I thought maybe an animal had killed it, but it had no mauling marks. I am just beginning to trust myself not to do things that make you upset. I should have left that bird where it was, but I was curious. Thought another animal had killed it. Tell me you are not still angry with me. I am a protector dog.*

Trinity

Other birds on the farm started to get sick and die. It seemed that the birds had acquired a disease from the rodents. Precautions were taken, and the disease was resolved. It was confirmed Trinity had nothing to do with the dead bird.

MAIZEE'S STORY

A few years later the owner acquired a dog from a puppy mill. Maizee's usefulness as a breeding dog had expired as she was no longer producing puppies. If a home wasn't found immediately, she was going to be put down. Maizee was a 5-year-old bulldog who had lived in a barn her whole life.

Maizee first communicates her living conditions before she was adopted into her new home. The adjustments were great, as her life of confinement had come to an end. Freedom and social acceptance from the other animals in the family were a challenge for a dog who had never known either.

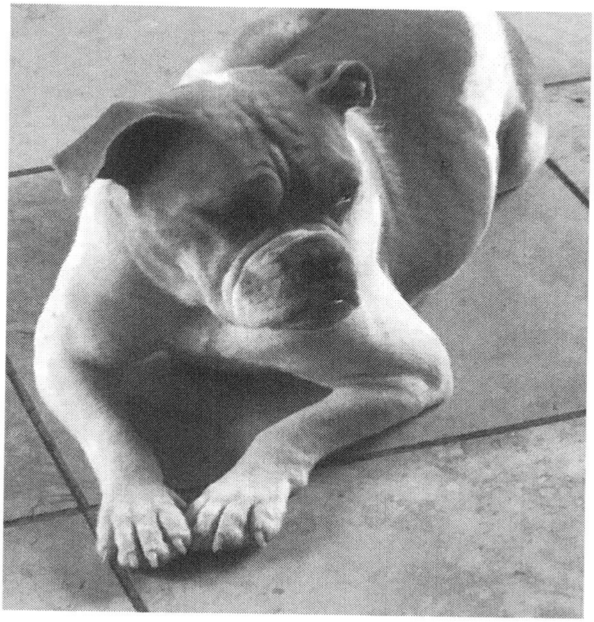

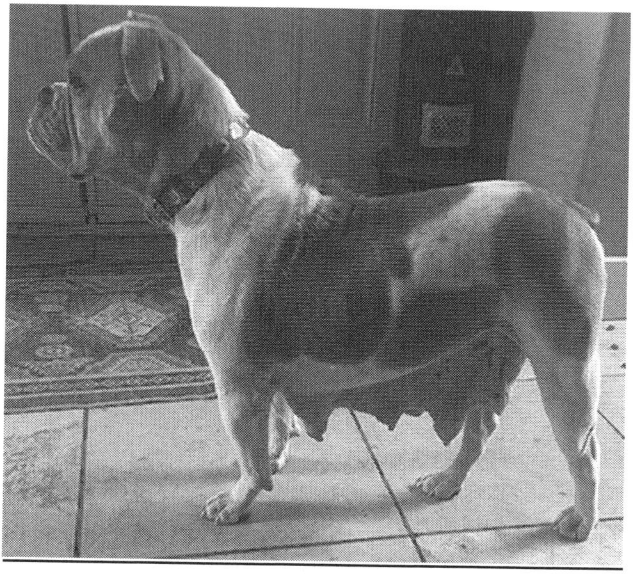

Message from Sophie/Maizee after Arriving at Her New Home

I feel lost but different. All my purpose that I know is to, time after time, have "squikly" little things that I have to feed. In the beginning, I wanted to keep them, look after them, protect them. This all I ever can remember. My purpose was to produce puppies. After a while, I tried not to care or be sad when they were taken from me. I was well-fed and looked after; this was all I ever knew. I heard talk that I had lost value to them; something wasn't right with the last batch. I didn't know what they meant.

There were two more like me that they didn't need. We were to be replaced by younger stock. We accepted what was to happen to us as it was supposed to be. Something happened. I don't know if that was what was supposed to happen. I had someone look at me—first time someone saw me. I was always one of a bunch, no names, just numbers, I was like 25, 125, I remember. They kept records, how many we produced, quantity, quality, something like that. None understood what it meant. The three of us were placed in a crate to be disposed of. It did not seem good. The other two were gone.

Why was I left behind? I did not know. First time, I was afraid, felt lost; nothing was as it used to be. I heard words spoken, different sounding than usual. This person looked at me, really saw me. Our eyes met. It had never happened to me before. I was curious, what was happening, all sorts of different strange things.

Finally, there I was with other dogs, not in cages, loose, running around. They told me they liked to play, then showed me fun. I didn't understand; couldn't figure out why they weren't in cages waiting for puppies to come out. I don't fit in, nothing like I have known before. I would like to stay; maybe have fun too, like them. I get tender pats like I am liked, kind of special. I feel quiet inside of me, maybe free, maybe run and jump, hope this stays for me. I will try to be quiet so it never leaves. I don't know my name, but I am happy.

<u>Second Message from Sophie/Maizee</u>

I was a number, statistic. As on all of the breeding dogs, this was their only purpose accepted as such. I am slowly understanding what it is you are asking me. Others like me showed no interest other than complying with what was expected of them. I was more alert, maybe smarter. I would greet the one that handled me, show her I was me, glad to see her.

Little bit only, she would pat me, all against the rules. She would sneak me out on a leash for fresh air, walk. She said nice things to me. I had become hard towards the litter I produced and couldn't allow myself any kind of protection for them as I knew they would be taken away. She always came back to me, many years, always kind. I started to produce smaller litters, some seemed quiet, didn't want me. I knew I would be replaced; she knew, too. She wanted to keep me, but this couldn't be. Her guardian father said the only option open was if she could find a home for me, not expecting she could. She told me all of this. This, to her, was almost impossible, but would not give up. Secretly, she named me Sophie, our secret.

I don't think she would mind that I tell you now. I am happy with either name, but now prefer the one you have given me. I am still afraid I will lose what is happening to me. The new name makes me feel this is her for me. Why someone can listen to me? I just accept. Maybe what I feel is happiness. I have only once felt this, my first litter, which I thought were mine to keep. The other dogs here are my friends, trying to teach me so much, sad of what I had been through. I miss the tenderness of my girl with me from the first I can remember. She was always there for me when scared. She would always talk to me from the first *litter time on. Tell me how beautiful they were. She felt sad for me to have them taken away. Later, it just became part of what I was meant for. The other dogs said I could do this, communicate, tell you about me, so I have, maybe again. So much to understand, know, but all help me.   Sophie, now Maizee*

At first Maizee seemed to adjust well to her new surroundings, then her attitude began to change. She, and the other dogs began to do their business in the house. Maizee started to kill chickens at an alarming rate. She would kill one then move on to the next, five at a time. She began to challenge and provoke Trinity every opportunity she could get. Trinity ignored Maizee's taunting, but soon the aggression between the two dogs escalated into violent behavior. When the owner tried to intervene, both dogs threatened the owner in retaliation. Trinity and Maizee were both given an opportunity to communicate and recount what had triggered a drastic change in their behavior.

Message from Trinity Concerning Maizee

This is Trinity writing, as I need help. I am losing it, losing it. All I have changed is leaving me. Maizee is wrong. She should return to her Creator as she can't help herself. She is making all harmony disrupting in pleasure. We will both end up returning home. I am losing what I have gained, going back to when I killed for prey. I had to dominate, killed to be over all animals so they would fear me. I am so afraid I will not stop next time she challenges me.

Once I taste the blood of victory, I don't know if I will be out of control, lash out at all in my path. Please do not let this happen. I was King of the Jungle; none would dare challenge me. Know, all of us prior were in harmony. I didn't need to be king of anything; there was enjoyment and respect for all of us. This dog does not understand respect and does not know how to accept kindness, love, or respect. How sad it is that she can't change, but she has been so totally wiped out of all goodness. Only our Creator can heal her. There will be retribution to those who have made her so.

I am sorry that I lashed out at my mistress, the one that loves, cares for us, but I was in a blind rage, unable to barely control myself. Send me back to my Creator before I give in to terrible things. If that happens, Maizee also.

Maizee is angry as she knows she is to be removed, given away; she feels it is my fault. If you get rid of me, then she can be the ruler. I have tried to make peace with all of us, have tried, but she thinks only her way. We would be peaceful together. Some jealousy may be there, but nothing like this. I protect my family. I nearly did what my maker would be upset with me, but nothing like I am upset with me. I can't redeem myself with Maizee. She isn't ready for this life cycle as she was so badly abused. She cannot get better, as within her are such strong emotions of hate for who made her like this. She will find peace on the

Other Side, release from all the blackness within her. It can be turned to the pureness that we were created as. This is not her fault. She was sweet, forgiving; in return, she was treated as the lowest animal, beaten when she no longer was of use. Angry at her because she could not produce. Forgotten food, water, until they could dispose of her with the others who had become useless to them. There is deep sorrow for her and also not for me. Understand.

Trinity

Trinity's Response to the Attacks on Maizee

QUESTION: What has Maizee done for you to attack her?

Trinity's REPLY: Maizee decided she was a leader, taught the others (dogs) to do wrong things. I changed. She should change, too. We are supposed to feel sorry for her, why? We all have had troubles; she is no different. She should not be here. This is our home, not hers. Go somewhere else. *We are a family, happy when she wasn't around.*

QUESTION: You were new once, and the others accepted you, your bad habits. Why not hers?

Trinity's REPLY: *She won't change, I know so.*

QUESTION: Won't you try for the family's sake? Please don't fight with her.

Trinity's REPLY: *I need more respect and love. I need this as I did change. I should have all of Maizee's attention. Ignore Maizee; I will leave her alone then.*

QUESTION: All need to get along. How would you feel if you were Maizee?

Trinity's REPLY: *I am not Maizee.*

QUESTION: You could hurt your owner if she tries to stop the fighting.

Trinity's REPLY: *Tell Maizee she is a terrible dog. If she changes, so will I. I changed; she should, too.*

Maizee teases us, makes fun of all, wants us to do wrong things. We don't want to. I am the only one to put her down. Others feel the same.

Questions to Maizee

QUESTION: Maizee, why have you started killing the chickens?

Maizee's REPLY: *I killed those noisy things as I wanted to. I don't like them. It made me feel superior that I could do it. I didn't know it was wrong, but I knew I shouldn't. It made me feel strong. I have never known that feeling before. I liked it. Just like now, I have made friends with the other dogs. This was nice. If you don't want to go out, you don't have to. See how I do it? It was funny. We all do it together. I am a leader; the others follow me.*

QUESTION: Will you stop doing what you know is wrong, messing in the house, killing chickens?

Maizee's REPLY: *Do I have to?*

STATEMENT: YES, this cannot go on. You will be gone.

Maizee's Response to Trinity

I am Maizee. I did do wrong things, made others do the same. So proud of the wrong things I do. I enjoyed being in charge. I think I don't want to be anymore. Trinity is angry at me, won't forgive me. I did wrong. Not sure if I will do it again. All were sorry when they hurt the mistress; extra work, not enough time for her to enjoy them. I don't know why I am like this. Freedom makes me want attention. Try all things, good or bad, just see what I can get away with. Don't know boundaries. Others say, especially Trinity, to teach me. Trinity teaches too hard lessons, knows ahead what I am thinking. This causes the problem

Message from Maizee a Few Weeks Later

I am unhappy, frustrated, angry. None of the other dogs like me. I got them in trouble. I don't want to be a leader anymore. I just don't belong. My history in this life cycle was not to do much other than supply one litter after another, be indifferent to these of mine that I nurtured only for a short time, then gone. This changed me when I became free. Couldn't find myself, know me. I have handled things wrong. I long to be cared for and loved but did everything wrong as I wanted everything: freedom, no rules, no holding back in everything or anything, not realizing the consequences. I felt superior. I could make everyone do anything I wanted.

I can't fight with all the dogs. I have nothing that I can vent anger, frustration at. Retaliation from the other dogs to make me follow the rules. They don't forgive me. What can I do? I go after those called chickens as they cannot fight back like other animals. There is *little satisfaction, but I still do it. I am so mixed up. I know I would be happy if I was the only, no other dogs. I would not have to share her with others. The other dogs wanted to show me how they all get along. I thought I knew better. Now, no one likes me; my fault.*

Maizee

Maizee continued to challenge Trinity. She would run up to Trinity and growl, provoking Trinity to attack. It was evident this issue between the two dogs was not only unresolvable, but dangerous. It got to the point where the two dogs could not physically or visually be around one other. A home was found for Maizee where she would be the only dog in the family. It was thought to be a perfect home for Maizee, however when the previous owner could not get in contact with Maizee's new family, concerns were raised. A writing was done and Maizee showed discontent with her new family. Apparently, there was an existing issue between Maizee and the owner.

Message from Maizee at Her New Home

QUESTION: Where are you, Maizee? Why do you not want to write?

Maizee's REPLY: *Do I have to?*

QUESTION: Yes! We are worried about you. Are you behaving? Are you happy in your new home?

Maizee's REPLY: *Kind of. Not pleasing everyone, but I am getting better. She, her, is trying, as I am difficult. I understand a bit more how to behave. They take me to a place where I am really happy; farm? Little girl won't let me stay there. She, her, tried to explain how happy I was, free there, open spaces. I want to stay there, best place I have ever remembered. She, her, doesn't want to talk to "K" (previous owner) because she doesn't know what to tell her. I don't want to return to all those miserable dogs who don't know how nice I am.*

I don't want to stay where I am as I know of a place I really would be happy. Little girl does not want to give me up even when she sees how happy I am on the farm. I don't kill chickens, do anything like that anymore.

Don't make me go to those awful dogs. I miss the man. We got along good but not good enough for me to return. Just leave me alone. Don't need anyone to feel sorry for me, as I can do that. They say I am spoiled. I am not suffering; I just know what I want, not what everyone wants of me. So there! Don't bother me anymore.

Maizee

It was later discovered that Maizee had been rehomed into another family. Maizee no longer wished to communicate. We could only assume everything worked out, and she found a home that was patient and loving.

Shortly after Maizee's departure Trinity violently attacked one of her household companions. The fight had to be broken up once again by her owner. This was quite concerning as Trinity had never viciously attacked any of her companions prior. It seemed that Maizee had an emotional effect on Trinity that had caused her to revert back to her old behaviors. Trinity was aware this was happening and felt she needed help.

<u>Message from Trinity Concerning her Behavior</u>

QUESTION: Why did you attack the other dog? You said the problem was with Maizee. Now she is gone.

Trinity's REPLY: *Trinity is me. I am still angry like I was before; I don't know why.*

STATEMENT: You were a protector, trusted; remember this. This is your last chance. Don't revert back.

Trinity's REPLY: *Maizee has mixed me up. She gets to go away, and I am here still upset, don't know what to do, still angry. Still Maizee's fault.*

QUESTION: Can you go back before Maizee? Think how proud, trusted you were to the other animals, to your mistress. Don't you want to return to that harmony and happiness?

Trinity's REPLY: *Yes, I remember, but don't know how I want to change back. I don't know if I can. I know you want me to try. Can you put me somewhere quiet by myself? Maybe I can heal. Something burst inside of me. There is another part of me I can't stop, can't think, I can't hold back. Even the ones I care so much about must stay far from me when I am like this. Isn't there some kind of medicine that would make me relax when this happens? I go out of my mind. Leave behind the good one. Help me to remember good. I don't know how to help myself; others don't, either.*

Trinity

Eventually through patience and understanding, Trinity re-established her roll as the family guardian. Her aggressive behavior totally diminished and once again she was the loving, obedient dog she strived so hard to be. `

Cooper – A Short Story

Cooper was an American Pitbull first purchased at 5 weeks of age. One year later Cooper was rehomed due to a divorce in the family. In his new home Cooper was constantly under attack by the other dogs. When the current owners of Cooper adopted him, he was extremely thin and nervous. He would whine and shake constantly. He had a torn ear and multiple bite wounds. Cooper wasn't neutered, did not walk on a leash, and was scared of men. In time, Cooper's true personality began to emerge. Today, Cooper is a sweet and kind loving soul. He communicates his past life cycle of abuse and how in this life he is surrounded by love and kindness. Truly a happy dog, with a happy life.

Cooper's Message to His Family
===

Cooper for family K, yes, I am beautiful in and out. Love does that. When they talk, they say I am a wonderful, loving dog, but that is because of the love I am given. My prior lives were not good. I was ready to be loved and to love. I tried to be good and obedient before, but all I got in return was threats of being whacked.

He was always angry, and I was the one he could take it out on. Finally, I did find anger and I did retaliate. Years of abuse, not looked after for even the basics of food and water, made me a dog I was not. I tried, tried, but then I was so hungry and thirsty. I was locked in and could not get out. When he opened the door, I jumped on him. I was put away.

I went into the light, the healing light, to recover. When I found peace and myself, I knew I wasn't like that. I was ready to try again. Sadly, I still took with me some of what I was like before.

Love, gentle love, kindness brought back such happiness. I jump with joy, beyond all hope. I have it all. I never want to leave this home. I don't have to tell you, as you know. Look into my eyes, and you will see all that. Within me is a spark that is so lit up with thankfulness. There is nothing I would not do to show this in return. My Creator allowed me another chance. I knew I was wrong to do what I did, but I know it is past, never to happen again.

Never leave me, as that would hurt more than the beatings did hurt. I know you wouldn't. As you can see, my love and happiness, abundant. All of you now are my happiness. I show it as it is returned.

Cooper

Myah – Here, Then, There

Myah had passed unexpectedly. At her time of passing, Myah showed no signs of being sick. Since she was a young dog, her owner requested a writing to try and determine what had happened to her. In conclusion, it seemed that she had ingested something toxic.

Myah's Message from the Other Side

This is Myah. Happy to do this as I do not want her to be unhappy. I am near often; she must know this. I was not very obedient, not because I didn't love her, but there was much fun I had to do, to try. I did things she didn't know I did. When she wasn't around, sometimes, I would chase the chickens and things like that. Never to do harm, just things for fun. If I could return, I would be better.

I can't tell her how I passed home. I think I did or was into something I wasn't supposed to. I write this as I feel this feeling. It just seemed like I was there, then right away, here.

My life with Mistress was a good life, a good time. I was loved even when I was bad. Not really bad, but doing my thing. We were close and will be together on this side. She will always be my Missy special. She had so much patience with me, and I felt she would be there no matter what I did. I am home now but missing her and our togetherness, friendship side by side. Our Creator knows she is special, but like me, not perfect, but special to me always. My true friend. Myah

Stewie – Final Message of Love

Stewie was acquired by his family as a pup. As a senior, Stewie lost his ability to see and hear. Surrounded by love his entire life, Stewie was torn between staying and leaving. His family requested a writing to determine his state of mind. Stewie narrates a message of love and appreciation for his family.

First Message from Stewie

This is Stewie, as you want to know my feelings. There is love, gentleness all around me. I feel with my heart I do not want to leave, but as my time draws near, I cannot delay what is known to happen. I know within myself something more awaits me. I feel love beckoning me and love holding me back. I don't know when it will happen. Don't cry or feel sad, as I am always with you. I think a different way than how I am now. I do not know or understand how my thoughts or feelings can be said, but feel peace within. I will pass from here to there with happy thoughts and memories, never to be forgotten.

Time is soon; remember me as I was happy then, even happy now in this passing. I have been with you before and we will be together again as this is our paths to cross again. The source of light for us is the same, as you know. You pray, and we pray our way. We have life cycles, as do you. We do not die but pass from here to there. When it is your turn from your life cycle, all of you in turn, I will be waiting as the happy pup you fell in love with.

Remember this as has been said, written down, not to be forgotten ever. You must let me go, as I am ready to pass on from love to love. You call me Stewie; pass this as a namesake on in my remembrance. Not, "Oh Stewie," just Stewie, your pet, thankful for the happiness you have given me.

Stewie

Second Message from Stewie near Passing

This is Stewie, a pet that has lived a wonderful life cycle in love and kindness. The joy of children, so gentle in their touch. My time is drawing near. Sad to leave my Earth family, looking forward to a release of what has befallen me. You have taken such loving care of me. Even though I knew I was a burden, I selfishly held on. You never complained; just made sure I was looked after. I know you will never forget me, and *you say never replace me. I am not concerned that you will have another pet. You showed me so much love that there is enough to share with others. You have taught me so much that I will take with me.   Stewie*

Stewie passed away shortly after these messages.

Baily – Why I Am the Way I Am

Baily was obtained from an ad on a rehoming website. Originally owned by a single mom trying to feed and care for her children, the extra pressure of feeding a large dog added to the financial strain. Most difficult was the decision to surrender the dog, a sacrifice for her and her children. Even though Bailey's physical condition was poor, it was clear she came from a loving home. Baily recalls her past lives to give her owner an understanding why she is the way she is.

Message from Baily

The chosen name for me in this life ended up as Baily. I have had many lives, many different names. We were created, as has been said, man's best friend. True words. These written words are what is heard all around me. I cannot speak but express as my Creator intended to communicate barks, yelps, cries, sometimes even tears, but the most precious is in our eyes; this tells all.

My prior life was lacking any kindness or love. I was like a trophy to show off. A very rare small ball of fluffy hair, prestige to show off to others. I was bathed, groomed, flowers, ribbons in my fur. When dignitaries and guests arrived, I was sent for to sit on her lap. No love, no kindness, just thrown down, ignored until I was needed again. I was spoiled, pampered, but that was not enough for me. I wanted to be loved.

One day, I was ordered, as usual, to sit on her lap. She said to get that despicable little rat here. I didn't know the word, but felt the hate directed to me. Revenge went through me. I had little bows in my hair to match her new silk dress. She was posed with me on her lap to greet the highly dignified socialites she wished to impress. Yes, I did, I let go a stream with all I could muster up, soaking her to the best of my ability. Joy sprung up in my revenge that had been cooped up for too long. My mistress could not dispose of me as she might look like she was the one to have the accident. She had to be gracious like that, uncomfortable remaining gracious to her guests.

My revenge was short-lived. The moment the door closed, she grabbed me by the neck and threw me against the hard wall. I felt shattered, like in many pieces. I was thrown out into the gutter in the rain and mud-covered, just looking like an unnoticed ragged.

This long story is to explain when I am upset, I still do this sort of thing; panic sets in. I am better now, as I know you get angry, but *forgiveness, love is always there for me. I have my own bed, but yours is more comfortable.*

Life before was also one that ended violently. I was just running along a wagon train and wandered off. Couldn't find my way back, remained lost for a long time. There was a farm in my sight. I was found by two children who hid me away. I regained my health as they brought me food and water. Times were hard on the family, little food to go around. Father was furious that they were going hungry to feed a dog. It was like fire going through me when he shot me. Traumas like this leave scars which take time to heal when you go home to the Other Side.

When healed, I was allowed another life cycle. This time, I was born with a litter used to a home having hardships. Some puppies died of malnutrition as she could not provide enough for all. I know some passed over, others given away. No one wanted me as I was sickly, not expected to live also. There was no lack of love. Being tiny, I didn't need much to sustain me, but as I grew, there was lack of food. I was always hungry. My mistress, out of love for me, decided to hopefully find someone who could look after me. I was not allowed in the car. I felt uneasy and scared. When I was put on a leash, it was handed to a big, scary man. I was so afraid, trying to make me small, shaking, confused. His eyes looked kindly at me. He took me home and fed me.

Everyone talked about my ribs—how skinny I was. That wasn't the problem; my empty belly was this they looked after. Now we are pals, me and "P," a closeness of love and friendship. Now you know my history. Our scars are healing together as we are good for each other. I know better, but when locked up or confined, I try not to panic, not revenge. I am happy to be loved and to love. Thank our Creator for allowing this happy time.   Baily

Firolais – The Shelter Pup

Firolais was abandoned when he was a young pup. He spent much of his early life in a shelter, adopted only to be returned. One day, a lady came and took Firolais to his forever home. A happy ending for a dog that only knew abandonment and human neglect his whole life. This is his story.

Message from Firolais

Firolais, they call me. I wish to tell you so much. First, I am the happiest one, as I am loved and cared for. You know this. When you carry me in your arms, I am so thankful to my Creator to allow me such gratitude. My Mary, we are so devoted to each other. I have lived many lives, some good, some not so. I wish to tell you this.

Before you came for me, I had such a different life. I was not even liked. The kids were good to me, but it was when they had time of remembering to feed and give me water. He less, but She seemed to hate me, called me an ugly creature, get out of her sight. I tried to win her love, tried to snuggle up to her feet, only to be kicked away. I didn't know anything different, so thought that was the way it should be. All of a sudden, there was a lot of activity, people in and out, the boxes all around. No one even realized I was around. The kids were too excited; He and She too busy.

Then, one night later, He put me in the trunk of the car. I was scared and shaking, not knowing why. A long time later, the car stopped, the trunk opened. I was told to get out. I didn't want to, as why was unknown to me, so he pulled me out and then drove off. I was really scared; it was pure black around me. I didn't know what to do or where to go. I cried, but that was useless as no one heard me. I slept, tried, woke up with sun shining, but nothing around me. My only thought was to go home. I ate garbage, any water I could find. Finally, I made it home. It was nighttime, so I just crept up on the porch, thankful, then slept.

I woke up to this person hitting me with a broom and yelling, screaming at me. I went away, didn't know where to go, so crept back to the porch I had known. This happened several times. I became stubborn and refused to leave.

Then, a truck drove up. A man with gloves on gently picked me, patted me and told me it would be OK. I was put in a cage. I did not have the energy to resist. I knew I was passing over and going home. When the truck stopped, I was so gently put on a table. The needles didn't even hurt. Ever so carefully, I was put in a cage on a blanket. There was food and water, but I was too weak to eat. I think I was fed, but I don't remember.

One day, I had enough strength to start eating, drinking water. All around me, dogs, cats, all well looked after like I was. We could play and run in a yard, not all friendly, but that was not a problem as I had made friends. One by one, my friends left. I didn't know why. People would show up to look at us. This one I like, oh, this one is so ugly. I then would try to hide. I heard my care people say this one will never be adopted here. What should we do? This was the first time since here that I felt scared. I was crated up, a long drive, then placed in a similar cage as I had been in before, food, drink, same.

Then, one day, this nice lady looked at me, I felt so good. Her eyes were so kind. Yes, this was my Mary. I knew our Creator had me wait for this special one. Does Mary know of my love, thankfulness of her picking me out? I try to show her every day as she does for me.

Our Creator's Blessing,

Firo

Second Message from Firo Explaining His Returns

QUESTION: Why didn't you tell us you had been adopted before and brought back to the shelter?

Firo's REPLY: *Don't tell Mary as I was not a nice dog. I will tell you what happened.*

When the lady looked at me, she said I guess he will do. Small enough not to be much trouble. I was so happy; they had a beautiful backyard. I soiled in the grass, so happy.

One day, after I had been there for a while,

I heard her tell her husband that she was upset. All her lovely flowers and shrubs were turning yellow. She was furious when she found out it was me. I didn't know I was doing something wrong. Her husband told her that I was just marking my territory; tell him to stop. This I did not understand. She caught me again after she warned me. I could not figure out why she was upset. I knew no different way to pee. I was returned to the shelter.

I had another time when I was so unhappy and continually disobedient, but I deserved to be returned. I just didn't know how to behave. No one showed me a different way to be until Mary promised I would not be returned; she was going to keep me no matter what. That helped me to understand the things I did wrong. No one had bothered to see I did not know how to behave. I slip up sometimes, but I don't want to. I love my Mary who took the time with me. Our Creator loves Mary, too.

Maddie – A New Life

Maddie was adopted after being turned into the shelter twice before she was six months of age. It was said she was too much, too boisterous, too large for each family. The first family had two dogs but chose to return Maddie. The other family had young children, which she continually knocked down. Indeed, Maddie was all those things. Maddie speaks of her last life cycle as a fighting dog. Her current life full of despair, never feeling she would find a loving home. But that she did; a home that showed patience and love, helping her to overcome her issues carried forth from her horrendous last life.

Message from Maddie

I have waited so long to tell you so many things. I don't know where I would be without your choice to pick me out of a deep depth of heartache and despair, unwanted, no love, not even kindness. Look at me now—beyond comparison. Do you know how my heart is filled with joy and happiness? I came into this life cycle with many problems from prior lives. I felt with no hope for any happiness. No one would ever love me or care for me.

Message from Maddie Recalling a Prior Life

I was the strongest, biggest dog in the litter chosen. I learned fast if I wasn't mean, I was denied food. I was whipped, mistreated so to bring anger, viciousness out of me. I didn't know why, but eventually, that is what I became if I wanted to survive to live. When I realized what was expected of me, there was no choice for me.

I was put in a ring, forced to kill or be killed. The only attention I got was when I was successful. My reward was the attention, the cheering when I won, good food after. Deep down, it wasn't me; there was always regret as to how I mutilated and killed my contender. I became old, I felt, and unable to defend myself. I experienced what I did to so many others, a horrible, shredded mess to die, unbelievable pain, seeing the victory in the eyes of the one victorious, what I had been. I returned to my Creator to be healed and made whole again.

I progressed so quickly, happy to be free to love and be loved. I was allowed to accept and work with a little one who had been abused as I had been. We bonded. A strong love and respect developed. This little soul I healed went on to heal and work with others who had been broken. My turn to return to another life cycle.

I needed someone to understand what mixed-up emotions were within me. I didn't understand, so how could someone be expected to take the time to find out? I was in despair; felt I would never find a way to ease what seemed to be still raging inside of me. I wasn't sure if I could put trust in one only to be rejected.

This, with me, has not been an easy path for you both, but you never gave up. Finally, I was able to release all the horrible past and feel the joy of being loved and love trustingly. Look what you have accomplished in me. Look what I have become. I can be playful. You say naughty, but I have the freedom not known to me before, a future that I look forward to each morning. I wake up with happiness. Another day to be so with you both.

Everlasting love I send you,

Maggie

<u>Second Message from Maddie: Name Confusion</u>

Maddie is OK. I am not Maggie, but Maddie. I can't know the difference. I hear Maggie this and Maggie that, my hearing is good, but I am not anything, but a dog, yes, named Maddie. Do you know how confusing this is? I am not perfect, and I really answer to both. I have confused everyone, even myself. It's like I hear Grandma, Mom, Great Grandma. How can I understand that? Even "S" gets mixed up. She calls me different names. I don't say I am sorry, as it is confusing. Not my fault; I didn't pick my name.

Your fault; name me different, "M."

Stella and Corona – Messages of Truth

Stella was adopted into the family before Corona's passing. Later, a new pup, Cayman, was introduced into the family. This story is narrated mainly by Corona. Corona speaks of her relationship with Stella, her past life cycle with her humans, then further explains how Cayman became part of the family. Corona's messages of love are all inspiring to those who love animals.

Stella and Corona

Stella

<u>First Message from Corona</u>

My name is Corona. I never thought I would ever be able to tell my mind in words. I am the happiest, loving pet possible in this life, not always so in past. I heard the talk about another puppy to be bought as I was getting older. I didn't feel old but knew this was a life that would end, and I would return to my Creator. I had no fear only was happy where I was.

I made up my mind not to have anything to do with the one called Stella. I looked at her and did not believe when I heard them say we looked alike, not possible. I always smiled as I was happy and loved. I was never like her, disobedient, always running around. No, we were not alike. I didn't even like her face.

As time went on, I accepted her as my own, passing your love of me unto her, my Stella. If my face is like hers, then now you know we were happy; everything droops. I must tell you there is no sadness in either one of us. Why our Creator made us look so sad, I don't know. He had his reasons! What I want to tell you, look into our eyes, see the happiness, the love, respect that is there always. Look beyond our faces for that smile as it is there. These many things written I have wanted to tell you, now I have. You know me; you know this is me.

My happy bowl,

Corona

First Message from Stella

This is my collar. I learned to really like it, as it now is part of me. Means walks, and you and Lady picked it out for me. I asked what is happening to my playmate. She doesn't want to run or even play. I don't want to hurt her as I am full of energy. I asked her, but she won't tell me. I am really upset inside as it doesn't seem right. Please explain to me so the hurt inside will go away. I don't want to hurt her either.

Stella

Second Message from Corona Near Passing, Same Day as Stella's Message

This is your pet, Corona, loved and loving my family. Inside, my spirit is good, but outside, not doing so well. It is our cycle on Earth that is causing me to feel like this. I understand this is my time; I can't fight it, so it will continue. I do not wish to leave my Lady and you, but it is my time to go home to the one who created us. This known to me; you call it different, but to me, it is just known.

Stella's upset, and I am not able to stand up to telling her. I will be right by your side. My love will allow me to visit you often. When you are upset or tired, I will sneak up to your side to share what bothers you. We have the link of love, always binding, never forgotten. Tell Lady I know she is always busy with that thing, but she always had time for me. Don't be sad. We had a joyous life together, always there, never forgotten on either side.

Goodbye, my good friend always,

Stella

Third Message from Corona after Passing

I am the one you call Corona. Thank you for taking my pain away and allowing me to come home. Inside of me is things that had happened before; we and Lady shared another earlier time. We had a bond then that carved over to this life cycle. I wish to tell you. It was many befores but so clear to me. I will tell you what I remember.

I called you Noble as that was what others said of you. You were kind to those that served you, around you. Everyone seemed to call your sister Ma Lady, so I called her Lady. She was so noisy her mouth never stopped moving. Noble and I would sneak away early in the morning, sneak in the kitchen for food. You rode your beloved mare, maybe something like Bridget (not right exactly). So much fun we hated to return home, us three, I alongside. Lady would be waiting for us, shaming us, many reasons. Her lips never stopped moving. What happened to your parents happened before my time. You were sister and brother, your house was big, so many humans looking after all.

One evening, we returned late, thinking Lady would greet us in her not-nice words. Noble walked into a thief, threatening him with a knife. Lady was tied up with a cloth in her mouth. The thief had a rope to tie Noble up but started to waive the knife at Lady if you didn't tell him where it was. You lunged at him to protect your sister, so he pointed the knife at you. Protecting you, I jumped on him. I killed him just as his knife went through me. I should not have killed him so cruelly, but it happened. Predators kill for food; I was wrong to do this. I passed over in the arms of you and Lady. I was allowed this special lifetime to undo the wrong I did.

    The one you named Stella is very young, she wants to see and know everything at once. Understand her as you did with me. I have told you our prior life together, so full of love as was this life. The ending with all around was sad but so nice. Know I am safely home.

Corona

Second Message from Corona from the Other Side

So nice to be able to tell you things now; it was more difficult before. We were close, and you always seemed to know my feelings. Why did you name a pet dog, female, with a name Cayman? She is not male, so I call her "K." Up to you what you call her. Sometimes, it may be thought a different name as you both are in for unexpected times with K!

There are many upset souls and animal pets passing over. We try to find and match up many so lost. We pets give kindness to all, but the little ones respond to our kindness and love as they can't understand what has happened. I am a kind dog, well-trained by a family in the ways of kindness. Much love, a closeness, not always there for all. This I am happy to have had in my life cycle with you both. Now, I can share this to others, knowing that is what is needed at the time.

Think, a little one passes over suddenly, no

one with no mother, dad. Yes, scared, crying. I am there as other animals do this, but I lick their tears away. Stay with them until trust, security comes to them. Together, we look for others they may remember. When they are secure, I greet others. My heart loves this. I will always miss you, as I know how deep you miss me. Don't you feel joy knowing because you both were so good to me, this I can pass on with what is needed by others? I am not so good at passing thoughts to writing, but you know it is from within me.

Stella knows when I am near, she wants me to come back. I am needed here but she doesn't remember this side, only we were friends. When there is a closeness as we were, I do leave an essence behind for you to remember happy times and me. K will give you many things to remember for sure.

Corona

Another Message from Corona

I did not know you didn't know about K. I will tell you. Because I am on this side, I see, remember, but K does not, like Stella also. We return to life cycles, each to learn different lessons to make us more pure for our Creator. I was through many life cycles, many lessons learned, that was why my way was better, could relate to your family. You know some of my lifetimes.

K was a very beautiful dog, had great pride in his ability to produce, sought to this purpose to have not only purebreds of beauty, strength. You will see sometimes two things about him, his obedience, his strength. He was a leader, stamina for running sleds, a true leader. He was so proud, the perfect Husky in all ways, very arrogant, pride of all the litters produced. He wished in this life cycle to overcome his pride, so chose to return to your family, knowing what was in store for him. Now, this did happen. He was "fixed." What could be worse than this to such a prideful dog that was known for his abilities? He is no longer, so to say, a male (man). What is he then, but female still not able to produce? He is now a she but still not able in any way to produce. The K or "Cay" is alright, but the man doesn't seem right. My opinion, but just that. We thank our Creator, praise Him.

See bowl and tooth,   Corona

Another Message from Corona, Further Explanation

This is Corona. I wish to explain better. I did not mean to upset you; write what I did and not explain. On this side, we are neutral. We were created to be a comfort, love, protect our masters. Disobedience takes more time. When back on Earth, we are so happy, new experiences, so full of life, joys of new things to experience. Humans are on a higher plane level. They have free will to be able to choose good or bad. The ability to invent, *drive a car, write, you know. The purposes are different, but both created by one Creator, our Father, God.*

Cayman was my friend, my buddy. We worked together, had fun, never apart. We planned that when my life cycle was over, then he should be the next pet to enter your life, family. I called him Fish Face; liked to eat fish. His name was Leader. From now on, Cayman will be a she. I really wanted to return to you, but we must have many lifetimes between cycles on Earth. She will be devoted to you and your family as I was. Stella and Cayman will be friends. Neither have remembrance of this side. Stella remembers me which makes me happy. Pets are never afraid to return home, only the sadness for the loved ones left behind. I have told you I am and will be the essence of my love and bond with you, family. I have always been a female. Stella, back and forth. Cayman always a male. Ask any questions.

Shine in the Light of our Creation,   Corona

Cayman

First Message from Cayman, Ready to Talk

I like my name. It reminds me of my prior life; strong, so strong, smart, pride in what I was. I now remember better things of the life cycle that I told you about before. I was the head sled runner, energetic with built-in instinct capabilities, even in the worst weather, always to get to where we were to go. Jake the trapper and me, a real team. I looked up to him. He was kind, honest, never cheating anyone, gruff but gentle, never let an animal suffer.

    The winters were cold, with blizzards, and snowed-in many times, but I was always able to lead the sled and trusted in my ability. I was sought after to breed litters, each strong, pure, all for sleds. I had developed self-ego; no other like me. The new Huskies strong, healthy, none others like us. There came a time when I became tired, Jake also. We did less routes selling furs. Trapping less, then more sitting in front of the fireplace. We were companions, always together.

    We were together on this side for a time; he has stayed. I needed a life lesson to bring down my conceit of how great I was. I knew what would happen, but I would have a good family to help me through an adjustment. Two things most, they say neutered, I am now. No Leader, but be like a house pet. Such a comedown, a good lesson to learn for me.   Your pet, Cayman

Cedar – Happy Dog, Happy Life

Cedar's story began when she was dropped off beside the road as a little puppy. Wandering around, scared and hungry, she was picked up and adopted by her forever family.

Cedar was a travelling dog. She resided everywhere her owner went. College residence, jobs away from home, no matter where the move, Cedar was there. An angel, she was not. Shoes, clothes, lipstick was all there for the taking. Her message is one of love and contentment, something lacking in her former life cycle.

Message from Cedar

It's about time you wanted to know what I think. My symbol is our home; we are a loving family with love all about. "Her" probably will want to renovate my picture of our home as is Her way. I call Callie "Her," my loving name just so. I don't like the name Chuck, so he is "He." I do have opinions, you know. I also know I am what you call spoiled. So be it, I like it.

I lived a different time under different circumstances. Different size, different situation, surroundings. I was, what you say, a prestige pet for show. That was it! I was groomed for show off. Well-trained to behave. All this and no love. I wanted someone to love me. It didn't matter how good or cute I was. It was only all for show, paraded in front of others, as I was a unique breed, very expensive, few of my kind. I tell you this so you know how I crave your love, enjoy being the center of attention left over from before, but the difference is love.

How happy I am. I have wanted to explain this to you, but is something difficult for my eyes alone to convey. My home, my family, I ask myself what more is this for me to ask for, nothing as I have it all, contentment and love. You know there will come a time when I will have to return to our Creator, but that is so. Let's enjoy every minute together, know we will never part here or there. Your spoiled brat, Cedar. God has blessed us.

Sadie's Walk of Shame

The family acquired Sadie after the passing of her owner. Sadie's dependency on her new owner was such that she would not leave the confines of the house when her owner left the premises. Sadie would get extremely anxious and fearful when left alone. Sadie was also having major trust issues with the male occupant of the house. In Sadie's writing she talks about how her past life has affected her current life cycle. The horror and violence from her previous life left her feeling guilty, unable to forgive herself.

Message from Sadie

Can you forgive me as I have been a terrible animal? Shame for how I survived. You ask as you don't understand why I am like I am. You think it is because I am scared? Hide so no one can see me. I wish this was so. I trust very few humans, as shame is deep within me. I cannot believe that someone would actually care for me, love me, hug and kiss me, trust me. When there is one that does, I can't let them out of my sight, fear that I won't see them again. Then, I will be all alone in my shame again, which I deserve.

A prior time, I ran with a pack of animals. There was a name for us, coyote, wolves, doesn't matter as we were vicious. There were no rules, love, respect among us, only survival for the fittest. We could turn on each other in a vicious fight to death. No loyalty to nothing, no one. We raided man's place, killed and ate everything, animals, man, not only as food but prey to satisfy a deep instinct we did not know or understand. They called it famine: no prey, no food. To survive, we turned on each other. Few of the others were as strong as me, so I was one of the last to be attacked for food.

I was awhile at home—Other Side—to undo this horror, then allowed to return for a life cycle. I am loved, hugged, made to feel special, but memories haunt me. I try to hide or make myself small as shame overcomes me; what I was, what I did. I am afraid of man as it was they who hunted us down with guns, shooting, killing us.

We, in turn, retaliated, killing them or whatever was near. I killed humans; now it is humans I live with, am loved, so cared for.

I am torn apart with shame. I cannot undo my past. Sometimes, I can forget when I run and play, but only with the one I trust. I feel man will turn on me for what I did to them and what they did to us with guns. I am filled with so much conflict, so I make myself small and try to hide. The special one that shows me so much care can bring me back. I need her near me all the time to overcome all my inside upsets. Now you know my problems, still love me.

The one called Sadie.

Sadie is slowly improving; however, after having her for over a year, she still does not feel comfortable enough to go outside without her owner present. She is slowly starting to gain trust in males and will only approach them for a pat if her owner is around. She is beginning to play with the other dogs in the household for short intervals at a time. Her owners are hopeful that she will eventually be able to live more in the present and overcome her past.

Gurdie – A Message of Love

Gurdie was four weeks old when she was rescued by her owner. Blind in one eye due to a severe infection, Gurdie never let that slow her down. Gurdie never barked, but made sounds to express herself to her owner.

Gurdie passed away after a confrontation with a muskrat. A writing was done to determine the circumstances of her condition leading up to her passing. Gurdie explained what happened and offered support and love to that special person she had left behind.

Message from Gurdie from the Other Side

I am so filled with sadness. No tears will bring me back to your hugs and love. The pain I was having made me want to go home, but now, with no pain, I want to return to you. Sadly, this can't happen. I must pass on, but this does not mean that I am not near. I can be near to you always; just ask.

It happened so sudden, so vicious an attack. I am not as agile or fast that I would, could defend myself. I was just checking out another animal; not mean, just curious. Wanted to maybe play. I knew I should have kept a space apart but didn't. I was not prepared for the viciousness of this terrible animal. I have been curious before, and it has always been friendly. Not this time! I should have been more careful, and now this has resulted in my passing on to home.

Do not worry about me as this is a beautiful place that I go to. Friends are there waiting for me. We will never be apart; just a little wait till we are together again. Don't cry; try not to be upset. I am well looked after. This is the circle of life that happens. We had an enjoyable, happy time, loved and fun. Think of this and praise our Creator that He allowed this special time together for us. I don't know all the answers to your questions but ask, and I will write again. Find satisfaction. I am free of pain, sad to miss you, but another home awaits me. Thank you for our happiness together. Your Gurdie.

Ellie May – 911

Ellie May was acquired by her owner when she was just a pup. She was always a loyal companion to her owner, loving and obedient. Ellie May always loved her food. When Ellie May had refused to eat, her owner became concerned. This had never happened before. Ellie May had grown extremely lethargic and nonresponsive. A writing was done, and the vet was called. Ellie May did not know what was wrong with her, but tried to explain her symptoms the best she could.

Message from Ellie May

How can I tell you what's wrong with me? I feel so tired, and my head hurts. I just want to lay quiet, so I don't hurt. I don't want to go home as I am happy here. I don't know if or what I did to feel this way. I need help, but I don't know what. I trust my Krista will help me as I don't want to leave. So tired, so sick. Stomach, I think. Hurts, hurts to go, like I have to pee all the time.

So sorry I am like this. So sorry, I don't know why. I am upset, but I don't want you to be.

Pray to my Creator,

Ellie May

The owner validated that she was unable to pat Ellie on the head without her reacting. Tests were taken as Ellie's abdominal area had incurred swelling. It was revealed that Ellie had advanced Lyme disease. Medication was administered, and Ellie May made a full recovery.

Message from Ellie May After her Full Recovery

I am Ellie May, happy I can write and tell you that I am your happy pal, maybe pet. I knew you would make me feel good again. It was like I was in a sleep, but not. I was not feeling things, looking from far away too tired to move.

Once before in another time I was sick, really in pain, different from this time, no one helped me to get better, no one cared. I wasn't sure what had happened, but it could have been when he threw me against a wall. I was easy to kick, picked up to see how far he could throw me, then call me to see if I would still come to him. He would pat me; I think he felt sorry he had been mean. If I could crawl to him I did. Last time I couldn't, I felt like broken all over maybe from all the times it had happened. I couldn't move so he just left me, said "useless dog." I knew this to be true as I could not do anything, He wanted me to follow him around, but I could hardly move or walk. One time I just whimpered in the corner against the wall, I hurt so bad. In his rage he turned on the young girl that was with him. He couldn't throw her like he did me, but he hit her, hit her, when she fell, he kicked her. I cried to see this happen as she was nice, kind to me, made sure I had food. I made up my mind if he had to be cruel like that it was better me than her. She told me she was going to run away but couldn't take me. She told me to do the same, but I was too weak, then had nowhere to go except back to my Maker of all. I was looked after healed on the other side, but it took a while. I wanted to be loved in my next life, accepted, then love someone. I wanted to be useful however as needed. All this I have now. I did not want to leave you in your kindness, and love made me good again. My love pours out to all the kindness and care around me. Walk in the Light as you shine.

Ellie

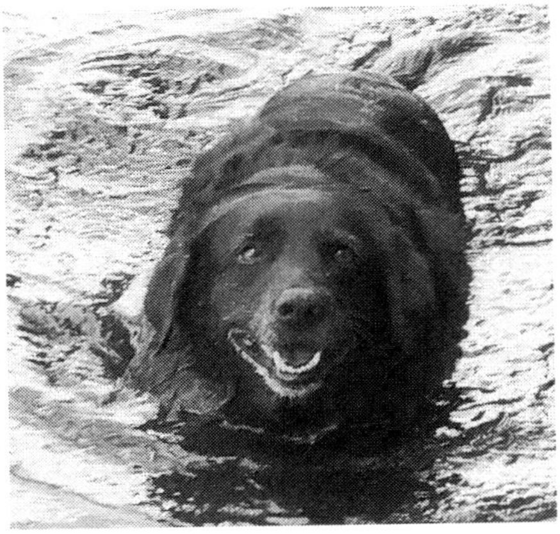

Zack and Ivan, Then Mexie

Zack, an Australian Shepherd, Dingo mix was adopted into the family when he was about 6 months of age. He was a fun-loving, gentle giant who always seemed to be getting into mischief. Even though Zack had passed away decades before, his family was curious to hear how he was doing. In his writing, Zack recalls some of his fondness memories, and how he enjoyed his life until his passing.

Message from Zack from the Other Side

I loved to chew stones. Why? Because I could not break them no matter how hard I tried; maybe a challenge! My life was happy, fun. My companion was a little white dog. I tried to ignore him, but he was always running under me, deliberately having fun. This I remembered most about him. I always wanted to do things; no stopping me. I was taken to some sort of training school. I did not like to learn to lead, be on a leash, or be told what to do. My solution to do this was to roll over with my feet in the air. Completely submissive. I won, no more training. I was quite proud of myself. Anytime I didn't want to do something, I used this trick, no leash, just free, full of fun, checking everything out. I did want to please my family, but I guess it was on my terms. Nothing stopped me from exploring the neighbourhood. One neighbour would take out his rage on me.

One night, I saw someone breaking into his

car in his driveway. I barked, carried on, waking up everyone, as to what was happening was not right. All the lights come on, scaring that person good. Best of all that developed was a good friendship with many pats and treats from him. I know I terrorized the neighbourhood. I got sick when I ate something hanging from a tree for the birds. I could jump high; strong and big was I. I snuck into a back porch as there was a nice turkey in a pot just for the eating.

    Sometimes, I did bring things home for my family. Package of meat, books, sometimes things that were put out on garbage day. Life was fun, I was loved, knew how to avoid any restrictions. I had a white dog at home. Ben, a dog friend outside. I got sick, could not

move. My Joe carried me outside as he knew I did not want to dirty the house. I heard them talk about my pain, crying as only girls can do, my family so sad. They carefully wrapped me in a rug to move me without as little pain. I begged with *my eyes to look at them once more, to keep that memory of them with me. I passed surrounded by love. A happy life lived. I tried to console Ben as he would not leave the front yard, crying, howling, all for the loss of me.*

We are friends on this side, romping, playing, nicking each other, all happy together, fun like before. My prior life cycle on Earth was all drudgery. Same type of dog, the job of herding, just work. If I became tired, I was whipped. I knew no love or kindness, only the job I was to do. I do not wish to remember this, but tell you so you understand me, why I enjoyed this last life filled with love, kindness, mischievous ways.

Remember me, k.

IVAN'S STORY

Ivan was an 11-year-old Maltese dog who, up to this point had been the only dog in the household. Zack, a boisterous puppy was not initially accepted by Ivan, but as time passed the two dogs ended up being best friends. Ivan's writing begins with him recalling a past life. A prize-winning dog, he was never allowed the freedom nor affection the other dogs entertained. In this life cycle he chose to be tiny and cute to get the attention he so desired in his previous life.

In his second message Ivan further explains his relationship with Zack and how Zack had saved his life. Ivan continues to explain about the lessons to be learned, and lessons to be taught for animals and humans alike, during their life cycle on earth.

Ivan talks about his passing, and his rebirth into a new life cycle as a female dog called Mexie.

First Message from Ivan

I am called Ivan the Terrible! Why? My prior life existence, I must tell you about.

I was a skinny, long-legged dog, a slim purebred. I was a ribbon winner, smart and elegant, with all the spots in the proper places. I was so well looked after that I was never allowed any freedom. Special food, nothing must mark me, had to be perfect. I never could just run, play, at freedom, always afraid I would do something to ruin my showing image. I was filled with jealousy as the other dog had all the fun. Cuddled, could do, go whenever, whatever he wanted to do. His nickname was Poopee. He lived up to this name. Accidents when he didn't like to go outside. He knew better. Naughty. Oh, it's such a small puddle; I'll just wipe it up, but no more. He was cute, always cuddled, always on someone's lap, brushed, ribbons. He could even go in the car, taken everywhere; people always stopped to pet him.

I needed attention, cuddled and patted, so I tried peeing in the kitchen. I do admit it wasn't like a little drop or two like Poopee. It was a bit massive. What an upset, so I did not attempt it again. Now, in this life as Ivan, I was determined to get all the attention like Poopee had. Cute I was, tiny, with long white fur hair, just like I wanted. But somehow, something went wrong.

The girls became too busy. I was ignored for boyfriends, horses, and another dog. I would be groomed, angry people trying to get tangled fur undone. Then, there was a special occasion; I went to be groomed.

Oh, how shameful I felt, I was shaved except for a little bit on my head. I hid, wanted to pass over, but nothing could be done. What I expected was that I would be showed off and admired. Instead, I was kept in the bedroom, away from everyone. Sometimes, I would be picked up and settled in a lap. Then, they would place me on the chair when they left. I couldn't jump down. I was too small and had to sit there until someone noticed. Oh, Ivan, do you want down? What do you think?

Things settled down, another dog, another cat, we were all friends. The big dog, Zack, got to run free and was his own Boss. Once again, I was never allowed outside on my own. The one time I snuck out, the dog next door thought I was one of his toys and grabbed me, shook me. It wasn't my time to pass over, but I never recovered after that. They gave me pills as they said my back was injured.

I liked my bed basket as there was less pain than if someone held me. I have no jealousy. I am told a lesson well learned by me, so true. Many good times are remembered, but this I have told you: love is better than jealousy. You know me now as Mexie. Surprise, but true.

Ivan/Mexie

Second Message from Ivan/Mexie

This is Ivan the Terrible again. There are still things I want to tell you. We had a happy home most of the time. We were Chez, the Siamese cat, two budgie birds, and me. Chez slipped into old ways, toppled the bird cage, and tried to eat the bird. The screaming, crying, yelling at him made him never go near the remaining one. I didn't understand why, but it didn't concern me!

What did, was a puppy came to live with us called Zack. Nothing was ever the same again in my home. He was so ugly, not like me, with beautiful white fur. He had funny eyes, ugly short hair, all different colours.

He just kept growing and growing; I was so small. I was afraid of him but as time passed, I knew him to be so kind, gentle, with so much love for all, even mean me. Sorry! I would jump in and around, under him, trying to bite his legs. He would remain still until I was tired. He would lay down, lick any wounds, and never ever was upset with me. One day, the neighbour's big dog, like Zack's size, thought I was one of his toys. His big jaws picked me up, shook me; it was horrible.

Zack came to protect me but couldn't do anything, so he jumped back and forth, barking furiously until everyone came running. Zack saved me, my always friend I didn't deserve. I still played under, around his legs and hid under him, but a fun game, no biting, just friends.

I became weak. They gave me pills to help the pain in my back. Special food. I think hamburger and rice were made for me. My stomach was in pain. The little girl would sneak my food out of the fridge. Mom would say to her, "Have you eaten Ivan's food again?" Mom made a double batch, so we both enjoyed it. Zack never ate mine, even though he was tempted. He loved me that much and tried to look after me.

One morning, no one was home but Mom. I was in my basket bed in pain. A light surrounded me. I knew it was time. I had suffered so much pain. Now, I was pain-free. I followed the light, and there I was on the Other Side, greeted with love for me. All were on that heavenly side. All of the Creations of our Father Creator. All have duties, functions, and atonements.

Lessons were to be learned when living the Earth's life cycle. Meanness, horrible acts against humanity, and animals must be atoned for. How? A learning process. First, seeing your positive/negative actions while on Earth. This is for all. This is difficult for humans as strong free will, the Gift of our Creator, has greater temptations.

Animals have a greater abundance for forgiveness as their spirits tend to be simpler for purity within. Those who dealt with wrongness must find forgiveness for themselves by seeking forgiveness from others that they have hurt physically, mentally. There is a natural knowing of what is right from wrong in our souls. All know this, but temptations are there, sometimes stronger.

You must wonder why I have written this. I have lived this life but now returned. A little dog again, similar as I was in the prior life. I now am different, old. I am between the Other Side and here. I am in a life now where I see nothing around me, cannot hear. There are gentle hands I trust that guide me, loving care all around me. This is a life cycle lesson for all, me, the ones that care for me. I do not concern myself but know it is a heartache for them. Soon, I will leave this life content in all ways. Difficult, but I know we will be all together again. As it happens, life lived, another life to live.

My Creator has allowed me to explain: a simple dog that has lived many lives to understand, explain the process of life, passing over, returning again. Animals all have special gifts which must be realized by humans. We can show them the way, loyalty, love, most certainly forgiveness. Our souls are pure until tainted by man but are always diminished by a loving hand. Believe it or not believe, I give you two lives lived. Created by our same Creator to understand. Ivan the Terrible, sweet Mexie now.

MEXIE'S STORY, PAST LIFE AS IVAN

Mexie was a Morkie pup adopted into the same family from her previous life cycle as Ivan. Now in her senior years Mexie had lived her life to the fullest. Unable to hear, half-blind, her desire was to spend her last moments with her family until she was called home. No regrets, she knew her time was near, but was grateful for the life she has lived.

Message from Mexie
==================

This is poor Mexie. Not really, as I am still here, loved, cared for. I do not need to hear or see as I have all here I could want. My time to return is drawing near. There is no fear. Others who have passed over are waiting for me. They have had this experience and try to ease the loss I will feel. They know it causes sadness for our mister and mistress, for me, but that is how it is.

I am a little pip squeak, but none dare challenge me without a fight. Not anymore. Content. I am to enjoy this time left for me here. I could not have lived a better life or found more love or kindness anywhere. My heart fills with sadness to leave, but know also my love always.

Mexie

Mexie's condition started to deteriorate at a rapid rate. In a one-week period she went completely blind. Unable to hear and see the owners made the tough decision to let her go. In her last writing Mexie describes what it was like for her in this current state, and how she was ready to end her life cycle. A very touching exchange between Mexie to her owners. Mexie was 17 years of age when she passed.

Mexie's Last Message Before her Passing

I feel thanks that I can tell you what I have happening. I am mixed up but will do my best to tell you. It is the darkness I don't know where I am. Gentle hands pick me up. Where is my food, water. They may place me where it is. Then the gentle hands pick me up, pat me tenderly then put me down. Where? I feel what I am on, the floor, but which way do I go. I hear no words, but know it is quiet. No movement, time to sleep but is it morning, I don't know. I dream, remember the fun times, jumping, barking. Everything was so good.

Only one thing I didn't know how to tell you I wished to make little ones, all my own to know they are from me, mine to look after, but it didn't happen. We all were such a good, happy bunch. We all just knew there was abundance of love for all of us, even the chickens. I can only live remembering this. I now wish to go to sleep, wake up on the heavenly side of our Creator. My friends are there from many times. I see the closest from this life clearly. I will be greeted, heal, be better, that is how it is, the time I can write this not to be sad but to tell you how much happiness you put in our earth lives. Joy will be ours when we all are joined together again. Let me sleep, when I wake up I am on the other side with your blessing.

Be happy for me.

Faith – A Jealous Dog

All souls return to a life cycle for many reasons, one of which to learn lessons and overcome imperfections created from a previous lifetime. Unconsciously all strive for soul growth. Just like humans, animals possess the same feelings of love, hate, fear, anger and jealously. Overcoming negative attributes is a common theme when reincarnating into a new life cycle.

In her previous life cycles Faith had always been the center of attention. She had never had to share the affection and love of her owners with other dogs. In this life, Faith was adopted into a household that had many other animals. Even though she is loved and gets her share of attention, Faith possesses strong feelings of jealousy which permeates into aggressive behavior.

When our animals experience anger, jealousy, or any other negative emotion, they may act out in frustration, trying to convey to us how they feel. In most cases, we do not equate an animal's feelings to those of humans. As a result, we may misinterpret their behaviour. Once humans understand this, many behavioural issues can be resolved with love, patience and understanding.

Message from Faith

I am upset and jealous. You keep bringing more animals home. Horses, I don't mind, chickens, OK, but not any more dogs. Zoey gets to go with you everywhere. When did you last take me with you? Never! I hear you talking about getting more. When will this end? There is less and less attention to me. Why are you doing this? Am I not also yours? I have such deep hurt.

Now, you are always angry at me as I am mean to whatever other dog tries to be good to me. I don't want their love and kindness; I want yours. Even though they try to be good to me, I don't want theirs but yours. So, there you know. Don't ask again!

Second Message from Faith

QUESTION: Why are you after the other dog in the household?

Your owner gives you equal love. She has tried to take you in the car but you experience motion sickness. No one to blame.

Faith's REPLY: *I told you don't ask again. The other dog is a goody goody always. I told you I don't like any of these other dogs only you. Get rid of them, I want to be the only one. I don't like to share you. You just don't pay attention to me* only.

When I was a Blue-Ribbon winner, I was the only one to be loved, petted, made a fuss over. I did not have to compete with any others. Why can't that be like that again. Just you and me I am special, deserve to be the only one.

Karma-Third Time's a Charm

Karma was obtained by her current owner from a backyard breeding facility. It was obvious that she had been neglected for some time as her coat was matted and dirty, and she reeked terribly of feces. Karma would shake uncontrollably the first few days on arrival to her new home. She was fearful and hid, preferring no human interaction. In her first message Karma communicates her previous purpose before she was adopted into her new home. Little hope, a feeling of despair as her litter numbers decreased, she felt no longer useful.

Not much was known about her history until her writing.

Message from Karma

I am Karma. I know my name but do not know why. I came into this life, not for sure why! The purpose was to have these litters, one after another. They were to be sold, all, not one to be cared for by me—a loss I felt within. My failure to produce these litters caused a problem that I was not needed, no use to them, money was important, no profit, no need to keep me. I was filled with fear, scared as I saw others disposed of, thrown away. Why? How, I did not know. How?

Why? Why?

It seemed it was my turn. A lady came looked at me; she said I will take this one. Again, I did not know what this meant. (second owners)

Yes, again, a litter of ones, not enough, not perfect. I always had been fed, looked after, but this wasn't what was happening to me. I was in some kind of shed. Others were with me, all just there, sometimes food, but so miserable. We all wished to return to our Creator. We remembered how wonderful it was on the Other Side. My friend, kind of, I think, looked like me. Her litter was born not moving, so they took her away. I think they helped her to go home. I had no fear if this could happen to me. There was no care, no kindness.

I shook all the time. I couldn't keep myself clean. The despair overwhelmed me. Time seemed long, just living, no purpose, no hope. One day, I was picked up, taken into the house. I was beyond afraid as it seemed then like she cared for me, held me. Then, some people seemed to decide they liked me, took me with them. I was frightened, but love, food, treats are all for me now. So happy! I try to forget "the before."

I remember when I was in a time before this. I was bigger, looked after many animals, kept them together, could not let them wander off. They were different than me, but I was told this was my duty, so I obeyed. I was seldom let in the house as I was to guard all at night also. That life was harsh. My life was short. This I know, happy to return home where I was loved, cared for until I healed.

All animals have a purpose, whether on either side. Many harsh lives can lead to another good life. This I have now. My purpose is to be special, love, happiness to one who returns this to me abundantly. I have found me, myself. Try to obey, but I surprise myself. I do not do what I don't want to. I will get better for love.

Karma

Months after initially arriving at her new home, Karma still did her business inside the house. As a result, Karma resided in a back room of the house during the nighttime hours. The owner noticed Karma was terribly uncomfortable in this room and did not understand why. Karma had her toys, bed and blanket, there was no reason, for Karma to feel such discomfort.

Message from Karma about Her Fears of the Back Room

I wished to tell you many things. I have found happiness, but fears are still with me. I am asked why I shake so badly when I am closed in the back porch. It is nice and cozy, I have treats, my bed; no reason to shake so. I will tell you.

It was a barn we were kept in. Many other animals, terrible ones. They were to be rid of. Poison, I heard, would be spread around. They didn't want some of us to get into it. We were shut up in a small area, forgotten, not always food or water, just so afraid. Those awful animals could chew whatever was in their way to get us. I escaped, she didn't. I tried to eat whatever I could on the ground but found grass, water, outside. I felt sick but felt better outside. My owner found me. I heard her say she had to find me a better life, a home. I think she liked me as she told me she was sorry.

Some of this I told you before. I was happy in my new home. Got scared again when I was taken away, separated away with other dogs, cats. I went to sleep there. I woke up in pain. Didn't know what happened. Everyone was upset with me, why I did not understand, I just wanted to go home (Other Side), stop the hurting. I almost made it home, but not my time.

I was tenderly cared for. I heard them say something that was what caused the problem. I don't like the back porch. There are many doors. I get panicky as I remember those awful creatures chewing their way into us, nowhere to run, no way to hide. Scared when I saw what they did to *the other one. She gladly returned home but such a terrible way.*

I see this when I am by myself with those doors. I shake with fear, do not want to stay there. I will be good; just find another place for me to sleep, any place but there. I know Andrew's door; no fear there, so I am understanding not all doors have bad creatures trying to get to me. You looked in my eyes with love, asking me to tell you. I like the kitchen, den, glass doors. I can feel safe. Porch has too many doors. No more back porch.

Karma

The total upstairs became accessible for Karma to choose where she preferred to sleep, no more back porch. She sleeps now for the duration of the night and seems happier, settled with her sleeping arrangements.

New difficulties were arising with Karma developing an attitude, we thought problems. She would not stay outside by herself. She liked to take her leisurely time outside looking around, watching the geese, the cars, not getting down to business. Nice weather was in her favour. Difficulties arose, when patience were short, and she diddled and dawdled with little heed for pouring rain or snowstorms. Not a problem except business was done in the house. A message from Karma explains her fascination with the outside. Never given the opportunity to be beyond four walls the entirety of her life, everything was new and exciting.

<u>Message from Karma Getting Down to Business</u>

Yes, again I want to tell you reasons why you must always be where I can see you. I know many of your words, the meaning especially the ones you say "obey, treat, inside, house then fun one, outside." I need someone with me outside. You say I am obsessed with cars; you worry if loose I will not realize the danger. This I do not know what you mean. Outside is not known to me before. I cannot get enough of what is all around. I sit and watch. Cars appear from nowhere then disappear somewhere. Other animals can be on the ground like me, then jump up, just keep going and disappear. I tried this but is a jump going nowhere only same thing, back. I understand water lake these animals can be on top of the water be near me on the ground then jump up and be gone. I watch with all my attention; can I do this. I look around me, I see no walls, where does all this go, end. Why would I pee and poo when there is so much, I don't know around me. I am used to dark, no fear as that is what I am used to, not too much to be afraid. I think I know the words to tell you how it is with me, so much I have never seen before. I get mixed up, need you near me, keep me safe. I call you Lady love RN write again for me I like it. Karma, Yes I am smart.

Poppy, Kona and Moseley

Poppy and Kona were two black labs that had lived their lives surrounded by love. Poppy had passed three years prior to Kona's passing. After Kona's passing, the owner was in conversation with the vet technician, who told them about a yellow lab that needed a home. Moseley was introduced to the owners, where there was an instant connection. Moseley is loving life to this day with the same family.

As the writing indicates, there are no coincidences. Poppy, Kona and Moseley had been together in previous life cycles. Moseley's life cycle with his family was already predetermined.

Poppy & Kona

Message from Kona and Poppy (2023)

This is from the ones you called Kona and Poppy. You think we would forget the wonderful life we had with you, your family, the love? Why? That is the most wonderful life dogs could have. Do you wonder what we are up to on this side? Work, work, work, yes! We had a good life passed in love, goodness all around, just like a warm blanket to keep us secure in passing. Going home to our Creator is not a problem, but leaving ones we love, so difficult. We left our essence for you to remember, remaining always with you.

On this side we have duties to work with others, people, animals the ones that have experienced trauma. They are in need of guidance, love, healing, in order to become whole again. Poppy had such a life cycle, abuse, neglect. I was there experiencing it; we were together. We were brought back to ourselves by others who were there to help us. When healed, we returned to a good life with good people, a Blessing for us, all the blessings and love we could impart from us to you. We tried to please you.

Poppy didn't like outdoors that much, but I was the happy one, outdoors or in, as long as I was with the family, my family. I would like to tell you Moseley endured a different Earth life and will tell you himself. When we—Kona, me and Poppy—arrived on this side, we recognized a friend.

Prior life, we three were together, running as a pack with others. Endured was starvation, cold, no human contact. We lived, we died, passing over willingly to return home to our Creator. These circumstances of suffering allowed us a better next life. How he longed to have love, give love, anxious to please but was uncertain how this would happen for him. We were so enthused to encourage him to join the family we knew and loved so much. This he did, your Moseley. He was our Gift to your family and you, never to waiver in his love, a companion like no other, loyal always. Kona, Poppy, remember.

Moseley

<u>Message from Moseley</u>

I wish to tell you my story. My friends of many lives together, good, bad to remember, decided for me where my next life cycle should be. So many good souls who loved animals. Where? Which ones should I choose? I wanted to be secure in love and loyalty. I had to give so much for someone, some family who needed this. Kona, Poppy, were silly dogs, enjoying all the attention that came their way. Happiness was all around. They wanted this for me, for their beloved family. They just knew I would fit the bill. Their sadness that they had to leave you, your sadness that they were gone. A solution was to be with this family. I had the temperament. I could draw the sadness of loss by a wonderful family to another dog, anxious to please, full of fun, run them off their feet with so much energy. That was me!

Animals, dogs especially, have deep emotions. They can cry, bark excited, warn of danger but mostly show happiness when happy, contented, secure. The abundance of love, forgiveness—unending. That is me, Moseley. Always full of fun. You see this in my eyes, anxious to make you laugh, sadness if you cry or are sad. Not so happy when I am not listening or into stuff; I still look like I am smiling. Now you know me *better, but I think you knew this already.*

Happy with bones, candy.

Moseley

Second Message from Kona

This is Kona. I have written about things you knew, but I now wish to tell you about now. What it is like on this side. What work is challenging, good to be needed and helping others. When we pass over from a happy life, we then like to help others to heal. Many experience terrible things that happen to them. This is true for all Creator's creatures.

I am one of many trying so hard to help a family that passed over in terrible crisis: a good family, parents with three children. This was new for me, usually just one human, animal, wherever I was needed. This is what we do between life cycles. Sometimes, we need someone to help us back. Sometimes, we can help others. A whole family, suddenly taken from their life. A bomb that scared them so violently, huddled together in fear. Gently, lovingly, now the children are guided back. When the children have started the healing process, then the parents can respond. Good parents to their children. The baby was the youngest, born to a horrible situation of war all around. Tiny, not enough food; she was very sickly. The caring hands, gentled, bathed her in love, slowly bringing her back to health, comfort, security.

I am working with the son, maybe four or

five. He laughs now, happy to throw a ball for me to bring back to him. He responded to me quickly. I am so proud I could do this, as I had taken so much with me from my time with you and my family. So grateful for this.

Their daughter was older, horrible memories will remain longer with her, hatred to those who ended her life so horribly. The parents are healing. The love they have for each other, their children, is beautiful, beneficial for the healings. There are many different ways of the healings.

Many souls are healers, teachers, counsellors, whatever is needed to restore lost souls. Then, there are many animals anxious to do their duties as needed. Top of the list are cats, dogs, even horses. Some may not be able to be reached by human contact. Fear, no trust. But a soft kitten or cat, yes, me, a dog, can win them. Their problem, that is within, some difficult to reach.

Poppy is over here doing what she does best. She is so full of fun, joyful, anxious to please, fun. The young ones passing over are drawn to her. She is quiet when needed, just a reminder that she is there for them. Moseley was a good worker on this side. You would be proud. Many have been brought back from despair, all negative situations, to positive. Some already back in another life cycle, just like him, renewed, ready to try again, lessons ready to be learned.

I hope I have reassured you all is well, happily for my Earth cycle family. Ask if you wish to, as I am always near telling Moseley to behave. Memories are beautiful.

Kona

Trixie – Not a Loss, Only a Gain

While on Earth, Trixie experienced unconditional love and happiness with her family. Once she passed, she was able to share this love with another "little soul" who needed to be healed. This is a perfect example of love being the healing center of all souls. Here is her story.

Message from Trixie

This is your pet, Trixie, named this while on Earth in your care. When we pass over, we return to our names we have on this side. My Creator allowed me to keep this name, Trixie.

I had known such happiness while in your care. I took this happiness with me and spread it to others who had misfortunes in their time on Earth. I tell you this so you know. Your abundance of love and kindness to all called doggies, pets, does not go unknown to our Creator. The warmth of joy you spread not only to your pets but to people around is a shining light. We were a good family, assorted, sometimes not bad, but what you called naughty. We felt guilty and wanted to do better, for we all loved you too.

Many animals, all kinds that God created, were meant to be companions to the souls on Earth, to bring out love, enjoyment, loyalty to who they were assigned to. Men, in their ego, felt animals were substandard and, as such, treated them badly. The forgiving nature of animals was to guide, be loved, but not mistreated. Do you see why you were so special in our eyes and in our Creator's? You were an example of how a companionship should exist, whether it be a horse, dog, cat. All animals deserve respect, as their heart beats the same for all.

Animals have no hesitation to pass over as they have trust in joining our Maker. Sad to leave you as I was. You wonder what happens when we pass over. Sometimes, we are united with a companion we had in a prior cycle, sometimes asked to be with traumatized humans, help them trust and find their soul again. Little children abused, neglected, need to trust again. This is where we are needed. It works both ways. Lost souls are matched with happy, adjusted, like us, to show them the way back. In turn, mistrusted animals find comfort in souls, people, that show them direction back to the fullness they were meant to be.

You wonder about me. I spread happiness what you showed me while I was with you. I am with a badly abused little girl who died at the hands of her parents. She cannot trust anyone, but now is trusting me. I can give her all that you have shown me while in your tender care. I write this in truth so you know and understand. Lift your sadness; not ever a loss, only a gain. I lie in bed with my companions sometimes.

Trixie

Second Message from Trixie

I wish to write more. Your heart would feel it is breaking to see this little one's abuse while on Earth. She has never known love, never enough nourishment, food, kindness and love. She is beginning to trust me but not people. I take her with me to visit you. I wish her to know the goodness that does exist. She cuddles up in our bed with the others. This was her first step of trust. She was accepted and fell asleep nestled next to my companions. The licks, kisses, and security were there for her. She has no name yet, so I call her my "little one." I imagine in your mind me and this "little one." Send love and prayers as she is beginning to see how life could be. You are the example I can show her. God's light shines upon you.

Your loving pet always,

Trixie

Eloise – I Choose You

Eloise was adopted as a young pup by her current owner. There was always a strong bond between them. When the owner experienced hard times, Eloise was always there for her. When Eloise needed comfort and security, her owner lovingly provided it.

Eloise and her owner had experienced past life cycles together. She explains one past life where she had been rescued by the same owner. The writing switches to the owner's higher self for further explanation of the situation, then switches back to Eloise narrating the conclusion of the message.

Message from Eloise

This writing is for my lovely Lady Christine. We are skillful with communicating between us, but there are times greatly appreciated to have the written word. I am intelligent but not capable; I wish it was otherwise. We have a special bond of love, friendship, but really a true respect for each other.

This life cycle was mine to choose. I chose

you. Why? You needed special hope, guidance to keep you on your path in this life. You know your trials and tribulations besetting you; I do too! Together, we can be strong. I by your side. Why are we so bonded? Many lives have brought us to this point in this life cycle. Many heartaches.

A prior life, your then father breeded dogs to fight in a ring, vicious in nature, against our Creator's nature. I turned out to be docile. Nothing caused me to retaliate. He starved, would beat me, sometimes burn me. I would just accept the torture, seek a corner to hide. Last time, I was beaten so intensely that I became useless to him for the purpose I was meant to be for him. You cried when you saw me. You begged your father to let you keep me.

Message Switches to Christine's Higher Self (Tranna)

His heart was soft for me, his daughter, spoiled. I usually got my way. This time, he argued. He would buy me any pet, but this one was not for me. I refused to eat. I would only stay in my room to get my way. Finally, he gave in. You were mine.

Fairly large, brown in colour, but the most beautiful pathetic eyes. You were mine. I did not trust my father when he took you away, but it was to try to repair the damage he had rendered to you. Always crippled, but that did not trouble me. I am Christine in this life. You are able to write this for Once Onana, as it was too traumatic to write. She now wants to continue writing.

Message Switches Back to Eloise

Yes, my name was chosen to be Onana, now in this life, Eloise. Your name was Tranna. You didn't mind that I couldn't run and play. You would just cuddle me, sing to me; we were inseparable. There are life lessons in every life cycle. My mind was almost completely removed of the brutal suffering I had endured. Now, beautiful memories of that time. My suffering, then his daughter's compassion, changed his very being, never again to do anything to promote dog fights. You, his daughter, had opened up his heart, humanity. I had many other animals he rescued. He worked healing, feeding, yes, loving these pure creatures, then finding homes for them. This was his way to redemption. All animals know forgiveness, then try to be better; maybe many lives to accomplish this, humans, animals.

You wish me to answer the question, why some writings are simple in words, expressions, other writings are just basic written words, really Christine?

Christine, you are so intelligent but not very smart at times, I think I am smarter. Accomplishing, developing an animal's word thoughts depends on the environment. Hearing, deciphering the sound, then meaning. Developing personalities depend on gentle pats, kindness, respect. Spoken words, we as animals are limited. Bark, cry, but it is our eyes that we convey our emotions! You know this, every moment, every dog, we communicate one way or another. Ask questions. I am pleased to give you my version, especially when I am smarter than you. That takes a bit of an accomplishment.

Lovingly,

Eloise

Baron – Let's Talk

Baron was undergoing treatment for cancer. His fun-loving personality had not daunted his spirit; it was all about fun! A writing was requested to determine his state of mind and how he was dealing with his current situation.

Message from Baron

This is your silly Baron, loved and loving my Missy and Dad. Yes, yes, I have names for you. You have a name for me; did you not think I would? So happy to write, didn't know it could happen. Now I can tell you things like you talk to me.

Missy, you look after me. I have not bad pain, but many things that hurt. I see tears in your eyes. Don't cry; I am well looked after. My family I care about, too.

I like riding in the car, but not always where we get to. One place I get scared, you aren't by my side. Nice, kind people, but not nice what they do to me. I tell myself, Missy must have a reason to let others hurt me. Sometimes, she tells me things I don't understand. I don't try to make a fuss, but I get really scared. She cries tears, then I really get scared. She tells me it is for my good. I don't agree, but trust it is so.

Sometimes I am tired but now feel good

again. When I am sick, I think it is my time to go home (Other Side). I cry; I do not want to leave. Now I know it is my time. I feel happy, anxious to play, then the walks. Food's good, but I want more of what they eat. This should be happening; that would really make me happy. I don't complain but thought I would let you know. I please you, so please me! Don't mean to be rude; I am a very nice doggie pet, well-mannered, but you know this.

I will tell you what you don't know, may not believe or understand. If you know this is me, then you will believe this. I was different in a different time, full of anger, hating everything, all men. I was big, kind of different fur. I fought other dogs, forced to kill them. He, my owner, told me I was a champion, top of the pile. I knew I had to do what he made me do. I didn't want to be vicious or go for their throats, but I did not know how to be different. I was kept without food or water before going into, called ring. Success was if I mangled the other one; the more blood viciousness, the more the shouts and screaming. I obliged as to what I was commanded to do. I became tired, old. I thought I finally would be finished fighting, but no! Horrible what I did to others happened to me. This I will never forget.

Now, I have a chance to be what I always wanted to be. Gently, kind, so happy. I know fun. My Creator knew my sorrow as to what I was. Granted this life cycle with a wonderful respecting family. I know pats, love abundant.

I know there is something wrong with me. I chose this as a way to ease my guilt for the horrible things I did, sometimes enjoying being a champion. To kill is against our nature; to enjoy it is wrong. I have explained, I have been given a joyous life but just a problem chosen to make up for my misdoings. I am learning to trust man again. Missy always. There may be worries. Ask, and I will write again. Your Baby Pet Baron

Chapter Three
For the Love of Cats

Chubby – From Past to Present

Chubby was born along with two siblings on a horse farm. When the farm was sold the kittens were to be left abandoned. The three were rescued by a woman who had boarded her horse on the farm. As time passed, Chubby did not overcome her timidness staying hidden, rarely leave the bedroom. A writing was done to determine the issue that had caused Chubby to be so fearful.

In some cases, when an animal is too timid to communicate telepathically, their companion friend will assist in the process. Maggie, Chubby's friend, initiated the conversation, and then Chubby felt comfortable enough to finish her story. Chubby shares her past life cycle of being attacked then dropped off. Chubby's past life is short but powerful.

Chubby

Maggie

Message from Companion Cat through Maggie

I am Maggie, loved, happy, told I am intelligent. That I am. My companion was not, wishes to tell her story. She is invisible to all except her caring, loving "T" and "P." Her story is difficult to start, so I am writing to begin. She wishes to be invisible to all except where she is, in a protective haven.

She was born, what they say, an alley cat, surviving on her own. A group of boys were hunting for fun but could not catch not even a rabbit when they saw her. They strung her up by her back feet on a pole. They strutted around until they were tired of the game. They dumped her on the steps of a crippled Lady, laughing—a cripple for a cripple.

Chubby Now Narrating Her Past Life

My Lady thought it was God-given to someone as lonely and forgotten as she was. Gently, she worked with my back legs, restoring them almost back to normal. We were happy together; no need to step out the door to cruelness. We would be curled up by the fireplace. She liked to knit; I liked to tease her and play with the balls of wool. Happy, so she would talk to me, sometimes crying.

Her mother was the mistress of a powerful man. When my Lady was born, no one wanted a cripple. Her mother eventually abandoned her. Tears would flow, and I would sit on her shoulder, trying to lick them away. We were close in our sorrows as I understood my Lady was looked after. Although she did not know her father, he still provided all the necessities of life.

A lady came in every seven to eight days with her son. Food, cleaning and washing were all looked after by an obligation of her unnamed father. Pride kept her from telling anyone she was becoming more feeble. One day, after her keeper cleaned, did duties, and her son leaving food, she fell from her wheelchair. The pain was intense. Her legs looked funny; she could not get up. Time slipped by. I could not help her; we cried together, her on the floor, me on her shoulder, licking her tears. I would not leave her, although she begged me to eat. I passed first, then her.

The keeper was guilt-ridden when we were found; no need as we were on the Other Side happy, whole, playing, but together.

Frieda – A Word to All

Frieda's owners were devastated when she passed away suddenly at two years of age. Two weeks prior to her passing, Frieda kept putting her paw on her mistress's leg like she was trying to tell her something. Frieda would also run, then suddenly stop and tuck herself in, looking lost and off. After she passed, her mistress held her body, and it felt like she still had her energy, as if she was saying, "I'm still here." The life energy remained until the time she was buried. An autopsy revealed she had passed from heart failure.

When animals/humans experience a past life cycle of pain and suffering, their next life cycle is usually one of love and kindness. Because animals, like humans, have the gift of free will, their chosen path may deviate. Instead of the healing materializing in life, it occurs once the animal or human has passed. In Frieda's case, she was surrounded by so much love and healing that she wasn't ready to leave. Now, on the Other Side, she recalls both lives lived.

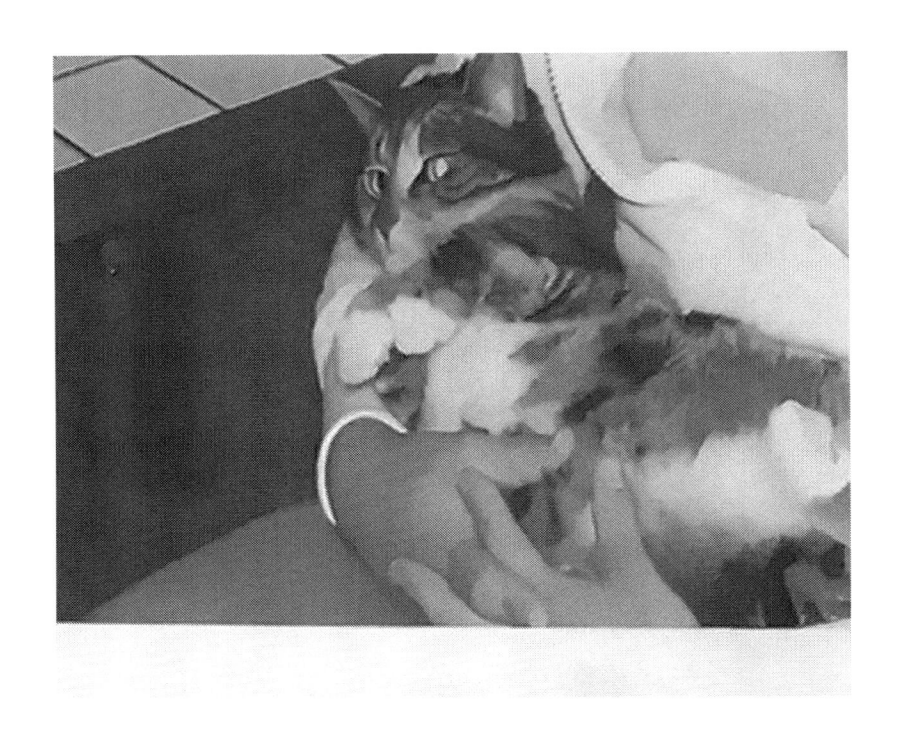

A Message from a Cat Named Frieda Margarita

Hi to my great people who looked after me so tenderly. I would not have stayed as long as I did without. If I had my choice, I would never have left you. You didn't know how unhealthy I was. Neither did I! I would just slip away for a rest, then feel better.

Why did you call me "Frieda Margarita?"

There was another name, but I wasn't sure I liked it better. Truly, you could have called me any name you chose; I would have gladly accepted it. Why? You were my special, special souls who looked after me, kept me alive longer with your love. I could not have asked for more.

Your Frieda Margarita

Second Writing from Frieda Margarita

QUESTION: Why such a generic writing? Could be for any.

Frieda's Margarita's REPLY: *You found out that I was an active one. Jumping all over, no care for anything, falling, breaking. I enjoyed myself. I had never been able to just run wild, no care. I played games. Pa couldn't catch me; it didn't matter how I misbehaved; I knew there was always love. I could always know I was welcome in someone's arms, laps; I just knew.*

A prior life left me so damaged, without

feelings, no understanding of life, not sure why I existed. I needed to know love, kindness, acceptance of me. This you provided abundantly. I was granted a short life to experience this, but didn't expect the terrible feeling of loss. I did not want to leave. I lingered longer than I should have. I did not think you should know of my prior life as it would make you upset. Now that I have known love, a beautiful life cycle, I can tell you.

I came from a dark place of fear. Only thing I knew what was happening, didn't know anything else existed. I was from a large litter. Well-fed to make us have lots of meat. I watched all being slaughtered to be sold for food. Animals understand this, but not the way it was done. Not only cats but all animals, sacred or not.

I was too skinny, but it was decided I was to be used for breeding. Time brought many litters forward until I became too old. I have such deep sorrow watching them being killed in front of me. I wished it could have been me if it could have saved them. I felt maternal to these ones I produced but hardened as time passed. I was thrown out in the streets to die, no use to anyone but with the terrible memories.

When I passed over, I was tenderly looked after to heal. I had never known love in any prior lives, but this one left me empty. They, my caretakers, felt a short time in a life cycle where I would be exposed to love, patient with me might help. There was a time limit on my heart. I was told this and agreed. I was not prepared for this, did not want to leave. Promised I would be good if I was allowed more time. I was to experience and know love, then return home. I stayed every minute, every second, fighting to not leave.

My heart broke seeing the anguish I had caused for you, Pa and T, but also for myself. The caretakers had to take me away as I would not leave voluntarily. You knew this. A heartache for you both and for me.

Our Creator loves all—animals of all kinds.

Torture of any kind is prohibited in any form, not for any reason. Brutal killing is not necessary. This is something that must be stopped. Humans must understand that animals would willingly return home if their dying had meaning, not in a cruel way. This is what happened. I will never leave you, Pa and T, our love and bond forever.

Frieda Margarita

Fee – The Fun-Loving Cat

Fee was a fun-loving cat, determined to have the best life possible. No slowing her down; she was making up for a past life lost.

Writing from a Cat Named Fee

Don't look at me and think you know me. I don't know or understand me, so there!

I was not a healthy cat. Still have problems, but I know I am well looked after; wouldn't be here if this was not so. This is the reason I want to check everything out. I don't mean to be disruptive. I do know that I push too far sometimes when I am in the mood. I know I am a me person, but I am only out for fun, explore; no stopping me. Even so, I am loved.

I know how to do tricks to get attention; I like attention, really! I know I am beautiful, a trickster, but why not? I can get away with this. Do you know why? Prior life cycle to this, I was like a statue; wasn't to move, just sit on my mistress's lap, looking groomed, ribbons, brushed to perfection my long hair. I was very unhappy but well looked after.

This life, if I lived, I was going to be a holy

terror, experience everything I wanted to do. No sorry, no excuses, just me. I know I am difficult, but I make everyone laugh. I know my routine; smart but funny. My family all love me. I show my affection for them. They know my love for them. After I was sick, I tried to behave, but I felt so good. I just terrorized my poor family, but they were glad I was better. I love my family. I am affectionate; they know this.

Fiero but Fee to them.

Carmel – Choice of Return

Carmel was dropped off as a kitten, and was living in a pile of brush beside the road. Many attempts to catch her were unsuccessful until one day she wandered and found shelter under the porch of the house. It didn't take Carmel long before she became an integral part of the family. Carmel is the only cat in a household with many dogs. Her writing refers to many short life cycles and her choice to return to a family she had once belonged to.

Message from Carmel

Carmel, the ruler over the household members of my loving family. This does mean I have established my authority over more animals than nails on my paws—joke. I do not lack for anything. I am beautiful, elegant, especially smart, and sometimes sneaky. Look into my eyes; this you can see. How did I accomplish this? My history over many prior lives.

Drowned as a kitten, later hit by a car. Then, brutally died from injuries from two boys with hockey sticks using me as a puck. You know this!

I was given this opportunity to enjoy a long life, a choice of family to come back to. Through my many prior lives, no one cared, showed any sadness of my passing over except one family: the tears, crying over the cruelty, bones broken, pain I was enduring. This was the family I wished to return to. I made the right choice. I have all, as the love and care that makes up for so many prior lives, short and sudden endings. Nothing will stop me from enjoying every minute I am allowed this life.

Many animals, but close to me, my friends are the dogs, special for each other, not perfect, but understand the need to be loved, cared for. I seem to be accepted without the jealousy competition that sometimes they go through with each other. I don't like this. I try to show them, by example, a peacemaker. There is plenty of love, care, for all. I try to stay detached from their conflicts. Altogether, we are a happy family. It hurts all of us if one becomes jealous; no need, but it happens. I wouldn't mind if no more would be added to the family. I am a peacemaker among all. I am getting old; would not mind less commotion.

I did have one long life so long ago. I was worshipped, catered to, my bed was of silk. It was a time of such elegance. My Lady was a priestess, worshipped in her own right. She never left me unattended. She believed I could predict the destiny; with her, we could curse those against her. That was a life of allegiance, luxury beyond belief. There was no comfort for me as her beliefs made me uncomfortable. She thought I was able to predict future, condemned those she wished to condemn, but I did accept all the attention.

I was almost God-like, but this should never have been. The beautiful jewels of my collar, more food than I could eat, always a servant there to anticipate my every movement. That time, animals were worshipped, gold statues in honour of them. Those who did not agree with my priestess were usually sent to the Other Side quietly. Poisoned, different kinds of poison for different ones, depending on how much she disliked them. I sadly accepted all this. That was why I had so many unfulfilled lives.

Now you know. A family, now secure, I love, and content in my choice.

Carmel

At a very young age, the owner had a kitten called Blueberry. The owner remembered Blueberry had been hurt by the neighbour's boys when they were playing hockey. Blueberry's injuries were so severe that she didn't survive.

Carmel's past life could have been a time in ancient Egypt, when cats were considered sacred animals and worshipped as gods. It was a common belief that gods took the form of animals, including cats. Cats were thought to be mystical, powerful creatures that could bring illness, bad luck, and even death.

Vanilla – A Transition of Love

Vanilla came to live with a new family after her owner had passed away. With the help of her deceased owner, Vanilla finally made the transition and is now happy and content.

Message from Vanilla

I consider myself very special. Not to brag, but this life cycle for me is a pretty nice one. I am beautiful, loved, can do what I want.

It was difficult for me to make the change from one to another Lady. I did not think I could live without my dear Lady. Marcy was so kind. Knew how I was hurting inside, missing my Lady. I couldn't understand why she didn't take me with her. Sometimes, she visits me, explained it wasn't my time; I had to carry on, but we would be together. She had to leave but knew I would be cared for and loved where I am now. She told me to be good, not naughty or cause problems. She was watching over me. Know when she was near. I relaxed, accepted the love offered me now, enjoying this special time with a special person. I am lucky, but it is the time before I pass over to enjoy. I love memories of prior lives lived. Difficult to bring to memory.

I was an alley cat, unloved and uncared

for. Little food, always having litters I could not look after. My heart was so weak it was impossible to carry on in that life. I asked my Creator to let me go home. I suffered so much in that life; that is why this life makes up for it. I would like to join my Lady but will stay here a little longer as it is so nice. Two special Ladies, all in a special name.

Vanilla

Chapter Four
For the Love of Horses

A Foal Born Terrified

We received these pictures with a request to explain the orbs and the cord that was displayed in the photos, invisible to the naked eye. The foal passed away hours after these pictures were taken. The foal's guardian from the other side explains the past life of abuse and why the foal chose to leave.

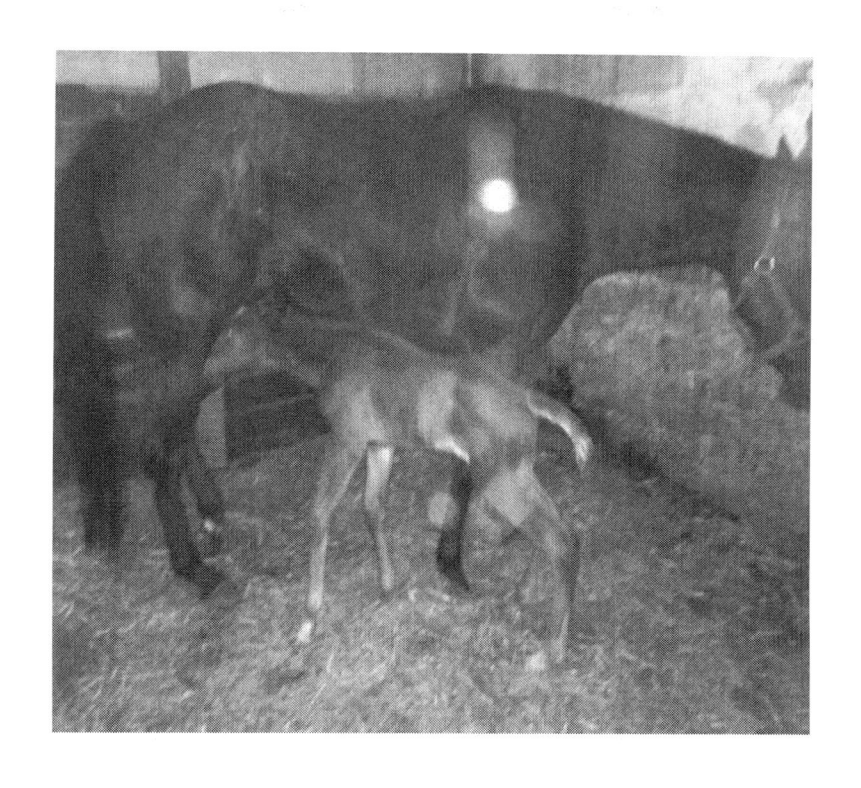

Message from Spirit Explaining Orbs and the Spiritual Cord

Connected to the Foal

First, you must understand that in prior life, inhuman acts were rendered against horses. This foal suffered greatly until the time she passed over in a prior life. She would not let a man near her. She was filled with such fear, afraid, skittish, just wanted to hide, let no one near her. Several handlers on this side tried to work with her (while on the Other Side). Patience and love finally brought her around to trust. Regaining enjoyment, running, eventually allowing someone to ride her.

Strength returned, confident that she would be able to return for another life cycle on Earth. Panic struck when she was born. She would not separate her umbilical cord, the one from this side. Gently, we worked with her to remove her attachment to this side. You see our orbs encouraging her to seek nourishment. We did try to encourage her, stayed by her side, never left her. Her fear overcame her, so we brought her home. We tried, she tried, but it was too difficult to overcome her fear, especially if a man was near.

The man who so cruelly abused her is now on this side (from her prior life). He wanted to work with her so that she would forgive him. There was no forgiveness, just terrified fear when he was *around her. We brought her home. Maybe someday she will return to the beautiful, trusting animal she was. I am her guardian; she trusts me always.*

When this filly foal was born, the man who owned the foal was present. Even though the owner was a different human from the one that had abused her previously, the foal was too fearful to stay in this current life cycle.

An autopsy was performed on the foal, and the cause of death could not be determined.

Flynn – Cause and Effect

An unfortunate reality is that Flynn's life is typical of many horses. Change of ownership over and over due to a misunderstanding of the horse. Retaliation and abuse seem to go hand in hand, resulting in a negative life cycle for the horse. Patience and understanding, asking the horse rather than telling, all make a big difference in the life of a horse. Flynn's message is clear. He initially wanted to please, but years of abuse from different owners made him an unruly horse. Now a senior horse, he has been provided a soft landing, a forever home surrounded by love.

Message from Flynn

This is a horse that began this life loved, eagerly wanting to please his master owner. I was, what is said, ungainly, awkward, not was supposed to have been made. My owner loved me, and together, my wanting to please him and he wanting to prove I was special taught me many commands. I felt I had become a splendid horse, obedient to his command.

When time went on, I was sold when he passed over. I did not know what a whip was but learned quickly. Being kind to me would have made me so willing to obey. The second owner was mean, and so I became mean also, which meant now he had a reason to punish me. I was so unhappy as I just kept changing owners. Not one treated me with love as I went along being sold, and I being angrier and harder to handle. I longed to return home, but I live a long life.

Now I know why! Before I am to pass, my Creator has allowed me to know love again. The happiness of being needed, being talked to, and hearing others in their upsets. Past lives have given many scars to overcome, but I am learning trust and feeling love again.

I would like comfort in my old age, but none of us are perfect, so I forgive these people. They do not know that I understand it is a problem to keep me in comfort that I demand but so wish for. I am sorry when I misbehave; just happens, then I feel sorry. I love where I am now and wish no other place to be until I return home.

I am improving, trusting and beginning to show this and love. Obedient I have trouble with but try. I know I am headstrong, they say, but because I am big and strong, this was my protection. Instead of fear from whipping, I caused fear. Now, I must overcome many bad habits. You will see a change in me, slowly healing and responding to your goodness. I am grateful for your keeping. The Creator's Blessings fall upon you.   Flynn

Dena and Liberty – Disruption on the Farm

Dena a 16-year-old Newfoundland pony was adopted by her owner, a lady who physically could no longer take care of the horse. Groundwork only, her new owner broke her, first to ride then drive. Never had she challenged her rider, always did what was asked of her. Dena was the type of horse you could put any rider on, and she would take care of them. Dena's first writing was from a content and happy horse.

Dena's First Message

I am called Dena. Happy to write to tell my mistress my love from deep inside me. I cannot show this like others, but it is there for her. When she is upset, I can only stand quietly beside her and pour out my hurt with her. When she cries, I also have tears in my eyes. My eyes can tell her all my feelings: sad for her when she is sad, anger when she is angry, just all like that. I could be better, but I am me, like mistress; it is said not perfect, but love and closeness is what I have to offer. She is a special being to me, and I know only kindness, love from her. Please find comfort in my words.

Dena

Then a new horse arrived at the barn. Sally was purchased sight unseen by her new owner as a quiet trail horse. It was clear from the beginning that Sally had underlying, unresolved issues with humans. Totally unprovoked, Sally would try to attack her new owner. She also would challenge the other horses, not just for social dominance, but to intimidate and provoke. It was clear the other horses were scared of this new horse. Integration seemed to be in vain as Sally would corner then viciously attack any horse that was housed with her. Dena's attitude and the attitude of the other horses began to change. Dena became unpredictable and agitated. Dena communicated her concern's and asked for help.

<u>Dena's Second Message Voicing her Concerns</u>

Something awful has happened to our happy home. We tried to make friends with the new horse. We all decided maybe we were jealous as so much attention she demanded. We thought maybe if we made friends, all would be back to usual. Our mistress did not see how she misused us. We are afraid of her (Sally/Liberty) not only for ourselves but for our dearest caring Mistress.

We learned she, Liberty, enjoys making us

feel safe with her; then, she goes crazy like she wants to hurt us or worse. She seems to have a power over us that we are not ourselves. We do things we would never do before. We are all sorry because we don't know why. We are scared of her and ourselves. We do bad things, and it is all we can do to not cause harm to the ones we care about. Why, we don't know. We have love, kindness and never, ever even thought of mean things to do.

Our happy haven not only is disrupted, but we are in fear for us, for Mistress especially. We know if Liberty hurt her, where would we be, where would our care be? We know of her love for animals, as we have had this from when we became hers, her love for us. If Mistress asked, we would not deny her to help another in need. I just say how we are! We would protect her even if it meant harm to us, but she must understand the cost to all. We are all sad, do not know what to do. Need help to protect Mistress. Ask Creator.

Dena, for all horses

SALLY'S STORY

Sally/Liberty

Message from Sally

Why was I sold? I am unhappy to have to start with someone new. True, I wasn't liked where I was, so I was mean. Maybe that was why they got rid of me. I feel angry, frustrated, so unhappy. I want to go home where it is peaceful.

Just leave me alone; I don't want to be good or bad, just me.

I don't think anyone is going to love me and look after me, but I don't want to hurt her. She looks tender at me, but I don't know if I know how to accept nice. Don't ask me something I don't know. I have hateness in me for humans. I don't know if I can trust any human person. I know I am mixed up and don't know if I will ever find peace. My insides are always in a turmoil. All the other ones seem to be content and happy; I am just an outsider.

STATEMENT: I asked Sally to be good and trustworthy, not hurt the one caring for her.

Sally's REPLY: *I hear, but I don't know what trust is. I am not sure of anything but hurt.*

My name is Sally.

Help was sent from the Other Side for Sally.

Message from Spirit

This is help for horse Sally. I am a horse lover who always helped ailing animals out of love and concern. This horse is unpredictable, "J" must be cautious until I can determine the extent of damage. I am reliable and sensitive to animals, especially those in need. Don't prejudge until I know what the problem is. From this side, we have more insight than any Earth psychologist. Do not give up, no negativity, as that will only upset her more. Love and kindness can do miracles. Ask me to write in three days. I will work with you as I know your strong love for animals. God's Blessing on all, no exceptions. I will reveal my name another time.

Second Message from Sally

I am called Sally. Can you call me differently? There is too much hurt when I am called this. I feel within me a loosening that maybe this is like home where there is only peace and love, never anger, only gentleness. Maybe this is home. I feel around me but see no ones hand soothing me, telling me not to be afraid or scared. Now, allow myself to be patted, even have treats.

I am told I am worthy to love and be loved. An animal of my Creator, proud, hold my head up for patting, not for strikes hitting me. This is hard for me to do. I am told I am worthy as I was created to have humans respect me. This feeling around I like. They make me feel different, accept the bidding of my mistress as she is all love and kindness, would never hurt me. I must never hurt her as she must trust me as I should her.

Inside me, is starting to feel better, then all of a sudden, I feel scared, dark scares me. I am told I will have companions and they also will show me the way. I don't know this, but it is said, in so gently a way, that it must be good. I only want to be safe. I think this must be home as I longed for so many times, a place to belong. I asked that this will be. I do not want to lash out anymore, as no reason to. I'm beginning to like my mistress. I hope she will like me. I will try.

Second Message from Spirit after Interaction with Sally

I have spent time with the one called Sally. She has been mistreated terribly in her life. Her last owner was always angry at her, called her names, actually hated Sally; didn't realize or care what was wrong or what had happened to her by the prior owner. The scars within will gradually heal, as the ones on her body. If you have the patience and love that I know you have, all will work out. Engrained in Sally is the horrible cruelty she had endured.

She saw the tenderness in your eye; that is the start of her healing. You still must be cautious as she does not know herself yet. She was denied food and water when trying to make her obedient, left in the cold, forgotten, lost, only cruelty upon cruelty. Having care will bring her trust.

She does not realize that is the problem as she has never trusted; does not know how, as all she has known from the day she was born, neglected in every way. Now, I have soothed her, shown her that love is finally there for her. She does not fully understand, cannot believe that someone could care and pay kind attention to her.

Be positive in your handling her, a bit at a time. Give her carrots, talk gentle and loving to her. After a while, do not rush; try riding her. In the meantime, walk, work with her. She likes soft music; even sing to her. Within, she is still like a young baby that has not matured or grown up yet, no experience, never schooled. Never show upset or anger anywhere around her. Why I say always be cautious is not from you, but something could trigger a bad memory. These will fade in time, but she is a damaged horse who will be reborn again under your love and patience.

Look into her eyes. This is a good way to communicate. Your eyes will console her; let her forget her past in your love and compassion. You both were together in another life where she knew happiness, was anxious to please you, the oneness of compassion, understanding without words. I will monitor the writing again. Caution, love, don't forget the treats.

Many Blessings upon you and Sally.

Message from Sally, Now Named Liberty

Why do you keep trying to help me? It makes me confused. I want to get angry, scare you so you will stop. I can't handle something I have never known before. But now I realize it is true. So scared to accept your gentle pat.

When I am angry, you do not punish me like others have; they call brutal. I have never known what you offer me with your extended hand, now from another with you, both gentle and patient. Can you understand how difficult this is for me?

I will tell you why. Others thought it was a joke. They would talk nice to me—what I so longed for—then hit me in the head, laugh at me. They did this over and over, accepting what I thought was true, sincere, then making fun of me. I could not trust them as that was their fun to try to get me upset and angry. Their greatest delight was to get me to bare my teeth, then run away, pleased with what they could do.

There has been no meanness after you pat me, just kindness in both from you. You didn't laugh when I threatened you, but I saw you were scared, I don't like you to be scared, and it confuses me. The memories are strong. I am strong and could hurt you, but would not be my intention.

There has been no one who cared to train me in any way. No one stopped the way they treated me, so I do not know anything different. I did not fear when I allowed him to pat me, so I am getting better, but it may take a while to overcome how they treated me. The hurt is deep. Any fast movement causes me to retaliate. Sorry after when it happens to you and him. This is me, not good or bad, but damaged. Now I know, not beyond repair. Don't give up on me, as there is love and a willingness to obey as I gain trust and respond to patience and kindness. I will be all you want me to be. The hurt and anger will disappear. I like Liberty.

Thank you,

Liberty

When approaching Liberty with the saddle blanket, she would get extremely aggressive, ears back, barred teeth, then try to kick. No sign of fear, but a dangerous threat of anger. Sometimes, when an animal has a traumatic past life, many of those feelings/fears are carried into their next life cycle. This seemed to be the case with Liberty.

Message from Liberty: Past Lives Remembered

The one named "J," I believe, needs to ask me why I am so terribly threatening when I see the blanket. How can she find out why? How can she help me? I panic. I believe something horrible will happen to me if I allow near or on me. I feel all anger to protect myself from something horrifying. I do not know what or why it is now causing me to react so. I fear that before I died in a fire, I could not get out of the building, maybe barn.

Every time I see the blanket, I feel like the blanket was on fire, burning me. I was saddled up, so I cannot understand how it could be on fire. I know I passed over in terrible, burning pain. I tried to get out, but everything was shut. Terrible panic, terrible, terrible pain. We were all on fire, burning the scream of all, even myself. I can feel the fire raging all around.

I want to belong to you. No other has bothered to try to find out what is wrong with me. I never want to hurt anyone, especially you two, but panic takes over. I know you are thinking of getting rid of me like all the others have done. I never cared before, as it just added to my anger and retaliation. Hurt others for what they so carelessly did to lock us in, to burn to death such pain.

Humans did this. She wanted to let the horses out, but he said it was more money for them if the horses were locked in. I think now he wanted to save the saddle but left the blanket in his haste to leave.

    Now you know my fear. I wish it would leave me so I could have peace, enjoy my new name, my new life. Now that I remember, maybe there is hope for me, I was never trusting. I know you will never hurt me. I never want to hurt you, but humans caused distrust, thinking to burn us for more money. I thought all humans were inhumane. What you decide to do with me, I don't know. Will I ever hurt you in my self-protection? I won't want to, but I don't know if determination on my part will help me to be reliable, trustworthy. I can't bring back any happy lifetimes, only meanness from humans, greedy with no regard of what pain they can cause. Can you make me whole again?

    I now can remember the bullying by kids for their fun with no regard to what they were doing to me, then sacrificing a barn full of horses to burn to death in the most terrifying way. I am truly damaged, but give me a chance to heal under your loving kindness.

I will understand if you and I have not overcome my terrors, hatred of humans, who have so thoughtlessness left me to suffer, not be able to trust, accept a helping gentle hand to pat me. You are good humans. I never want to hurt or see fear in your eyes. If it happens, get rid of me.

Liberty, like those oats.

Resolving Liberty's Issues, Remembering Good Lives

QUESTION: As you remember the terrible fire and the meanness of humans, can you forget? Can you remember a life when you were happy and content, and had good humans who loved you, rode you, patted you and told you how much you were loved? If so, do you want that again? Can you be trusted not to hurt anyone in retaliation for who mistreated you? Tell me, please.

Liberty's REPLY: *Yes, long ago, two children loved me. I was their special friend. When they were young,*

I was included in tea parties, dressed up with ribbons and flowers, even a hat. So happy, so complete a life. They could climb all over me, cry tears all over me when upset. Ask my advice; I was part of them, from children to grownups. I even lived long enough to see their children, who took to playing with me their games. I was so gentle, trusted, even with the very young ones.

To receive the gift of trust is precious. This I would like again. If I can hold onto this memory, and it is a strong one to overcome my terrors and distrust, this is what I would want. Just to feel the touch of a young one telling me their stories, singing to me would strengthen the good memories against the bad.

You asked and now I tell you as I remember. I am not sure if it would help, but that blanket triggers horrible memories. Would you hang it on the wall for me? Put flowers, ribbons, a picture of little ones. Would this override the good over the bad?

Music all around me singing, little voices telling me their stories is what I remember. When I passed over, they all sang to me their favourite songs, from the littlest ones to the ones all grown up. Some were silly nursery rhymes but so cherished. My eyes fill with tears now that I can have these memories back.

What I was and what I have become is not pleasing to me. I ask our Creator to forgive and help me return to what I was, not what I have become. There was not a moment of distrust that I would hurt one of their precious children. Put pictures for me of children and horses showing love and respect. I must dissolve my hatred, replace it with the gift of trust for all. If I cannot disperse the anger and hatred with all the good, happy remembrances, then home, I must go, willingly, where I can be healed. Remembrance of all good things I knew is the happy life I want to replace the terrible. There is good, loving humans. I know it is here where I am; now it is up to me. I like flowers, ribbons, music, singing, telling me problems, all to remind me.

The one with the nice set of teeth to forget.

I want to tell you how tolerant I was of children. My teacup was a bed chamber. A bowl used under the bed to be used for nighttime peeing. Most unpleasant, especially filled with lemonade. How could I refuse? It was a tea party I was part of.

Memories are flooding me. This is good; I feel my heart lifting.

One time, I was all dressed up in ribbons and flowers for a special occasion. My tail was braided with great difficulty by the children. I was paraded around for all to admire. Some of the ribbons ended underneath my tail. I couldn't hold it any longer. Yes, I did it, everyone's horror. The children burst out laughing, and it was a fun moment that did not last, as they had to clean and remove the ribbons.

Just nattering, nattering, why didn't I go sooner? Horses can enjoy all the happy, fun times children can think of. I was their "Merry Berry." Who else would gleefully name a horse such a name? When I start getting into bad memories, call me your Merry Berry. I put up with their pet name for me, but I like Liberty.

Liberty for life.

Message from Liberty Trying to Forget

This is Liberty, a horse fighting for a new life, free from all the horror I have experienced. Patience and understanding have been extended to me so generously. This I accept without reproach, eventually. Any reminder brings memories of suffering because of

fire. Bringing to me memories of happy times will eventually put in place the horror ones.

I do like music, but what is that called that you have had me listen to? Makes me jittery. I can't get enough of the affection shown to me. Memories of the little ones always hugging and kissing me. Their tears when things went wrong. As these children grew up, their many tears over boyfriends.

If they did not like horses, animals, they were gone. I was always chosen if a decision had to be made. No second chances for them! I only knew gentle hands, from tiny and to the gruff one who looked after me, brushing, having always perfect for the girls, then later the boys that were sired from them.

"M" reminds me of the one who looked after me. Even when I was willful toppling pails, things that a young pony gets into mischief. I liked to chew things. Never, never was there a severe reprimand. M reminded me. Feelings hurt, but knew I did wrong. I want to be friends with M. He will not hurt me, but he lets me know wrong gently.

Since that happy time, I have not known peace, happiness within me till now. I have my home. I will try not to have memories causing me to retaliate. Think I must protect myself from unknown forces. I must remember there is no danger, pain that I must protect myself against; only warmth and love surround me. Go easy on the blanket. The memory of it burning into me is still very real.

You spoke of many things to me. I hear all;

I listen. I love your attempts to sing and talk to me. A healing process, a soothing path to recovery.

What's with the dead flowers? (Plastic flowers were hung at her stall.) I only knew fragrance and live ones, then withering gone. I don't mean to be difficult, but maybe that was what was around for me. My happy time never knew cold or snow. Because you do this for me, I will enjoy what you have provided, flowers.

I send my warmth, gradual love to the two that are now my refuge. Recovery for me is slow, but I know I am protected from all harm, memories. My name reminds me I am free from old memories but still be cautious.

Liberty's behaviour started to digress, her horrific memories proved to be too strong.

<u>Message from Liberty One Month Later</u>

I am beginning to get back horrible memories. As hard as I try to bring, the peace and love you are giving me just isn't working. The fire, my memories are just taking over. When I remembered my children's love, it came back to me. Then I thought I could change, trust, accept your patting, kisses, just like when I was happy, content.

Things bring back memories so horribly hard to overcome, not that I want this to happen. Both of you are my good humans, but sometimes you look like the bad humans. Something triggers the fire, blanket burning. It scares me. When you come near me, I want to hurt you, so I try to get you to leave me alone. You keep looking more and more like the ones who set me on fire. I think you remind me of the smoke all around me, then the fire burning me. I was the last to die, so suffered the most. I cannot erase the burning fire, then the hatred of humans.

You gave me for the first time in this life a

few times of a happy, peaceful, pain-free time. If anyone could have erased these bad memories, it could be you both. I have written before if I cannot put away my memories and hate for two wonderful humans like you, then it is best you let me go. More and more, your kind faces are being replaced with the bad humans.

Something causes this. I smell smoke, think fire is going to engulf me, then want to hurt others for my painful existence. I do not want to carry on anymore. The thought of going home, the thoughts of peace, free from anger and hate that is within me, healing. I am feeling that I am getting out of control with no way back to hope for something I can't do. Should I hurt anyone, I see things like fear and anger tramping down. My hoofs in the air scares me. I don't want to be like that.

Before this happens, as I get worse, you must replace me. Let me go home to my Creator. I may return to you again after I am healed. Your *memory will stay with me. We will find each other. The joy of a reunion, special, as it is worth waiting for. This will happen. I know we were meant to be together, if not this lifetime, the next when I am healed. Return me to those who sold me to you. You and I were meant to be together for a brief time. Some happiness was there to be remembered. Now, put me back on my path back to my Creator.*

Libby was sent to a farm shortly after this message, where her rehabilitation moved forward. She currently lives with another rehabilitated mare and belongs to a loving family. We examined all the factors that would cause her to digress, and we concluded that the owner, who smoked at the time, may have triggered the past memories of the fire.

<u>Message from Dena Once Liberty Had Been Sold</u>

This is Dena, well looked after, well loved. I

am asked, will I behave? I want to, I will. I had upsets when a new horse came to stay with us. I had trouble getting over the meanness of Liberty (Sally). I felt very confused how this could happen, why our mistress would do this to our happy barn of animals. We all were friends, then to have to put up with meanness from a new horse was so confusing. I blamed Mistress for doing this to us. Why would she? Was she not pleased with us? Why did she buy another horse? So upsetting.

It took a while to realize it was not against us; she still loved and cared for us. She did not love us less but much love for us all. The new horse was mean to her as Liberty was to all. We were happy to see her go but sad for our mistress, our mistress, who was also upset and in fear of Liberty hurting her. We listened to her, felt her concern for such a terrible animal, but not wanting to put her down. We knew her deep hurt as we were hurt also. It took time for us to heal.

Now, all is good again. We will try harder to

please our loving, kind mistress. She looks after us so well. We will try to do the same to her. Sorry, but hurting. Did not mean to misbehave. Good now.

Dena

Since this message was received, Dena has indeed changed her attitude. She is no longer spooky and unruly. Her calm, sweet demeanour has returned. The atmosphere in the barn returned to the way it was before Liberty had arrived.

Diva – Past, Present, Future

Diva was a quarter horse mare who passed away years ago. Diva and her owner were inseparable. Diva would be saddled up and the two would hit the trails. No matter what they encountered, fear never crossed their minds as they were bonded in trust and love. Diva's owner requested a writing to see how she was doing on the other side.

Message from Diva from the Other Side

Diva, Diva, Diva. I love the sound when you say my name. I love all animals also. On this side, we have duties to do. Because I had known such love, kindness and consideration, that is what I passed on and helped abandoned or mistreated animals. There is a terrible saying, "mistreated like a dog." Terrible, as our Creator made animals for companionship, to be respected, kindness and love. We were like that, you and me, but all are not so.

I enjoy what my duties are on this side. They say it is called rehabilitation, returning suffering mistreated animals to the rightful places as God intended. The love, joy you gave me is always with me, cherished. What you don't know is we will be together again.

Also, we have had many life cycles together. That is why we are bonded so close together. Sometimes, love is once in a lifetime. You will find another horse to care for and love. There will be a bond, but not as close as we are. Just because you are there and I am here does not mean the bond is shattered. No, it will never change for us. When it is your time to pass over, we will enjoy our riding and fun times. You will help me. Together, we will work helping others by example. Give hope to mangled souls so in need of comfort and love. A human and a horse working together to show others what can happen when they can forgive their tormentors.

Terrible things can happen, but like all Creation, love is there for all. More difficult for some than others to find. You cannot look or find one like me or the same bond. Opportunities are there for you. You must understand there is a duty to work with animals who need help, security, and love will be returned.

We are special, you and I, but you should show what you can accomplish with one in need of your attention, your skills to help them. You cannot replace me, but make me proud if you can help an abandoned animal to know how much love is in your soul to share. On this side, I see so much heartache.

Sometimes, a soul is in such need of love. I will stand beside them, there for them to turn to me. Animals are meant to bring comfort, loyalty; humans should return their companionship. Animals are so special and should be treated as such, always forgiving. A lesson for humans to learn. When damage has occurred, our understanding hand should be extended in gratitude, respect and, of course, love. This is what this side is all about. No animal is afraid to return home. We will meet again. I am near.

Diva

Belle – The Horse with an Attitude

Belle was purchased sight unseen, advertised as a quiet, broke trail horse. Contrary to this, Belle was extremely green under saddle. It turned out Belle had a little bit of an attitude. She did not like talking to the communicator afraid her attitude would be exposed. Everything was on her terms. As it turned out, Belle had many unresolved issues.

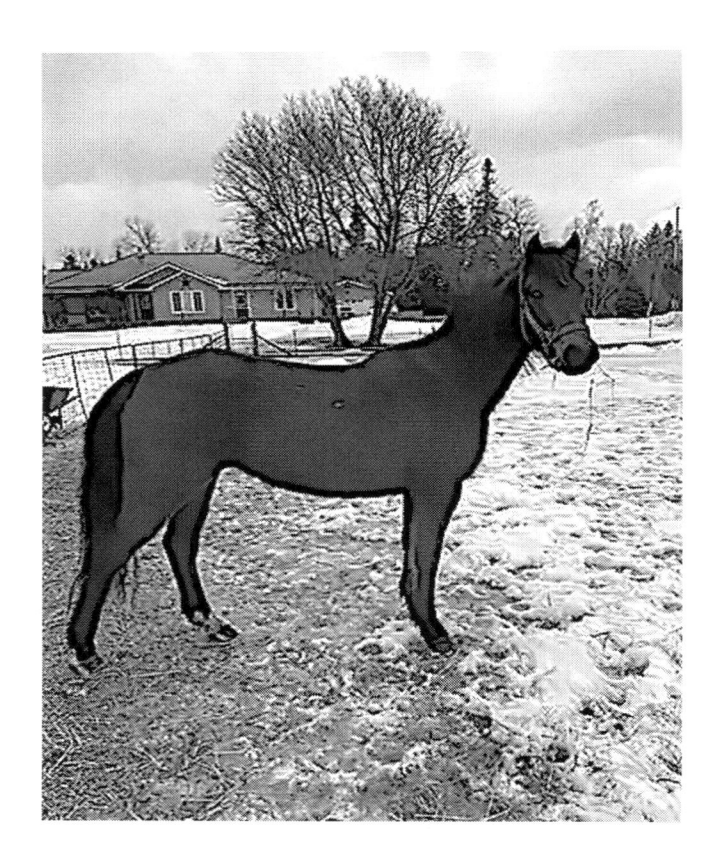

Message from Belle

I am the one you call Belle. Don't care for Jade (new name). You wonder about me, what I think, want to do. I am neither here nor there, so do not be concerned. There is no part of me that wishes to be different. You treat me kind. I know I am a bit different as horses go. Just the way I am. I don't like to have someone rough with me. I can't respond fast as it doesn't always happen that I know or understand quickly.

At a young age, I had an accident. I heard said I was a young foal. I was to pass over, but not my time. I recovered but was never treated as nice as the others. I made up my mind I would be better. Tenderness, love, you have shown me. I do not want to be sold ever; just find a home, not where I am ignored. I am smart but a bit slow. I can love if I am loved, cared for, understood.

In a prior time, I was abandoned, became lost, cold, hungry; no food, only snow. I was helpless, alone. Alone, I fear this to happen again. I look at you and wonder if you will become tired of me; look for a better horse. You talk to me, then I feel secure. When you leave, I get upset, but you always come back. I have no reason to doubt my existence, but I have feelings of fear, doubt, scared to overcome. You are the nicest thing that I can ever remember. Don't change, but I will try to overcome what happened to make me so. I do respond to you, your patience. I am not disobedient; just take time to understand. I will overcome what happened before, enjoy what I have with you now, look ahead to what I should know: a loving, comfortable tomorrow. I didn't like you cutting my tail for someone else, but have figured out why. I like my bales of hay dry, lots of water, treats, but not snow. Green grass, patience, love you have shown me. This I know.

Your Belle

<u>Second Message from Belle</u>

I wish to write again. I have not always

been a good horse. I don't like you (to the communicator) because I do not want it to be known. They say I have an attitude problem, so you know, don't want you to know more. I always blame another one, but not me. I will blame you. Although writing is an opening for me, I didn't know existed. My attitude may change as you are not a bad person trying to disgrace me. Sometimes I will have you write, but first I must be secure in my new home. This is how I am. I don't want to ruin what I have now.

QUESTION: Why did you write tail instead of mane?

Belle REPLY: Don't like you. Return it to "S," not yours!

QUESTION: Anything else you indicated wrong?

Belle REPLY: None of your business. I will let "S" know what name I pick. I just don't trust you. I will let you know when I want to talk to you again. Maybe call me Angel, so that will remind me to be pretty good horse. Angel (Belle)

Bree and Donkey

Horses can have personality conflicts with other animals. Often, when these conflicts are present, they can fester and affect their relationship with humans. In Bree's case, she had trust issues with a donkey on the farm. She became fearful, and her behaviour erratic. She soon realized there was no reason for her distrust and decided she would try to think before she reacted.

Message from Bree, the Horse

You ask me why I can't be friends with Donkey. I am not sure, but I feel if I trust her, she will turn on me, be mean. I try to be obedient, trustworthy, but I have a mind of my own. I remember a time when I was free to roam, free to run, I did not have to obey any human, conform to their demands. Sometimes, I do want to please, and then I want to be free, run, be wild.

Donkey is strong to me. I just do not want

anything to do with her, I wish she would just disappear, and then I would be happier. I heard the words that I would be given time to improve, then I would return to the place I know best. This gives me unrest. My spirit feels lost, not belonging anywhere. I know where I am now should make me feel secure. There is kindness here. I am uncertain within to relax and allow a companionship to happen, with human, with Donkey. I go between wanting to please, fear of what I don't understand and outburst to vent my fear as a protection to how I feel inside.

You ask me to trust Donkey, as there is an offer of love and companionship. There is no reason not to accept this friendship; no more being wild or afraid. I will try to think before I react and realize there is no harm to me. I do not like the name Bree.

Stella, Chance and an Angel

When connecting with Stella and Chance, the owner's guardian angel/guide offered a message of love. We all have angels assigned to guide and protect us; this particular angel took the opportunity to let the owner know of her existence. Chance and Stella then communicated their messages. Stella was unrideable, and the owner wished to understand why.

Sometimes, memories of past lives can affect the current life cycle of the horse. Abuse from the past can evolve as fears in the present as the animal remembers the physical pain to their body. This seemed to be the case with Stella.

Chance

Stella

Message from Owner's "Guardian Angel"

This writing is for "H," but first, I wish to address her. All will be written as asked. You know me not, but I am always near. I guide and protect you. I also know all, as I am like your Guardian Angel, always true to you.

We see the love that flows from you, generous to all, whether others or animals. Do not be hurt easily, as you are a kindred soul to be cherished. You walk in our Father Creator's Light. Now having this written for you, I can commence with your questions.

Message from Chance

The one Chance has a deeper meaning than just a word. I am satisfied in all you do and say to me. I was so mistreated in a prior life. Now, I bask like the warm sunshine, loved and cared for. What more could I ask for? Oh, yes, treats. Look into my eyes to see the love, respect I hold for you.

Message from Stella

Stella, as I am called, finds it difficult to trust. Many problems are mine, so difficult to deal with. You are like a bright star glowing with love and understanding, even you do not know what my problems are.

I have come to this Earth from a prior history of beating and abuse. I was not to bring this memory with me, but it sometimes happens, as in my case. Bones were broken, the pain I endured then; some have remained in this current state. If I am to heal, it will be my Creator's wish, as you are the one to help me. I do not mean to shy away as it is the remembrance of injuries I sustained before. Your kind, understanding love for me is a healing force I have never known before. You can do no wrong, only glow as a beautiful healing soul.

I have not known the freedom I experience here. Just get carried away in my wanting to experience being not so good, attention knowing

I won't be punished. I will try to think before I do, as it is not intentional to hurt you. Maybe a little discipline might not hurt to remind me that it is destructive and that I do not want to hurt you. I will be your friend, companion, as I am happy I am with you. May have to wait and see, try as I will behave. Ask to write again; this I enjoy. Praise of our souls to Him that created all.

Stella

Second Message from Chance and Stella

This is Chance, you haven't asked for another writing so I will do it for you. I am secure, happy, and content under your loving care. I have a companion. We don't always agree, but we are learning to respect each other. Some faults were due to jealousy. We wanted to be your only one. Now we understand you have enough love for both of us!

Stella would like us to ride together, but

injuries I had in a prior life make me shy away from this. I don't think I still have the injuries, only the memory. To please you, I wished we could ride together, but fear stops me. I think I need to be trained to overcome these fears. I am doing better not to be so destructive, but I still have a bit of me that wants your attention.

    I also get bored. I need some challenges. Teach me; I am smart enough. I need someone to overcome my fears, trained, disciplined. You are too kind to do this for me, too gentle. I tell you this as I would like to please you. Walking around with you at my side gets boring. I want to run, yes, ride together, as I hear your wishes; they are mine also. I do not like to say this, but I need some strict rules, or I will become more spoiled. Need challenges, really, please. I have written again just for you to know me better. You are my full life now. Blessing for you from our Creator.

Oliver – OOPS, Let Me Stay

Oliver, a senior horse in his late twenties, had been moved to a boarding facility when the owner of the farm passed away, and the farm was sold. Oliver heartbroken, believed that he had been given away and asked to be taken home (other side). Shortly after, he developed Pulmonary Pneumonia. A writing had been requested at the height of his sickness. A year later, new problems developed, and another writing was done.

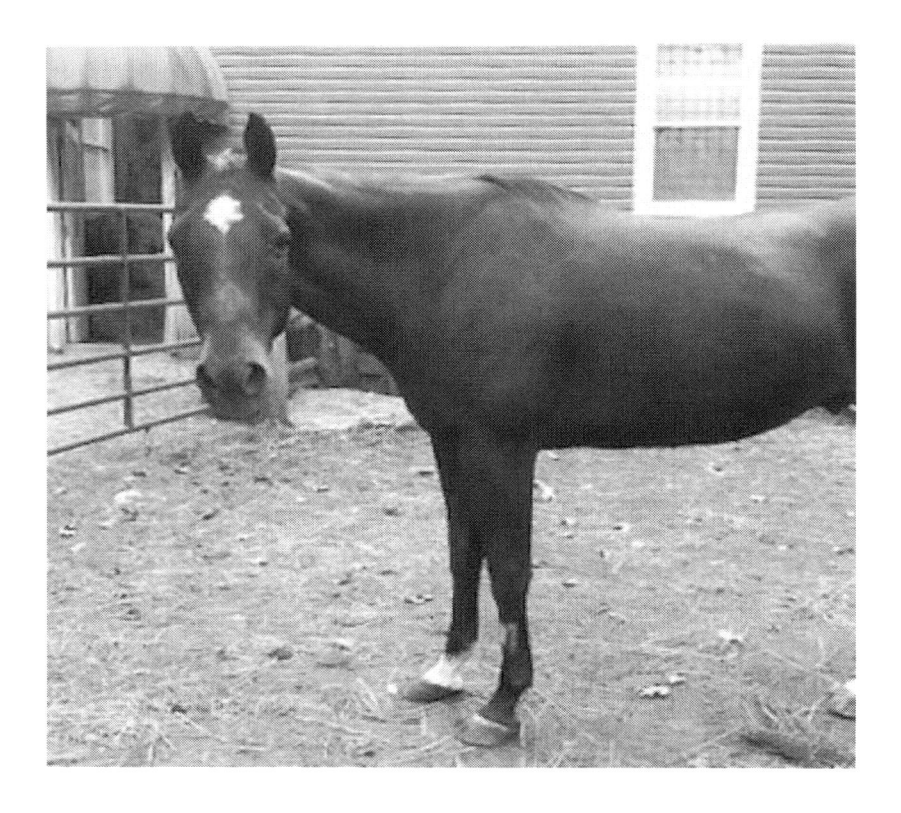

Message from Oliver

Oliver. The hand that patted me, loved me, cared for me. My heart broke when she gave me away. (Oliver was only moved.) I wanted to pass over to home. My Earth life had been full, happy. I asked to be taken as I could not see anything ahead for me. This happened; I was given a choice to pass over, too late.

I found another with care and love like I had experienced. I did, do not want to pass over. How could I have been so foolish a horse? I should have known that I would be well looked after, as my friend "R" would never allow otherwise. I so hope it is not too late and I will be able to remain now in the care and love I had known before. It is not like I was abandoned, forgotten at all. Now, I not only have one but two that look after my welfare.

Such a blessed horse that should have never complained but lacked trust from those who loved him. I hope I am able to overcome what is *happening to me. Care and love, I feel. I cannot leave; I do not want to leave. Old I am, but hopefully, more time will be allowed on this Earth for me. If not, I have known two beautiful souls I will never forget. Just imagine that. What horse would want to leave even to return home?*

Our Creator's Blessings are there for you,

Oliver

Oliver recovered from his sickness, enjoying his senior years frolicking with his barn buddies.

One year later, Oliver stopped eating his food, and his body condition started to deteriorate. A writing was requested to try to determine what the issues were concerning his loss of appetite. A spirit helper first communicates that Oliver's pain was making him depressed, and wanting to go home.

Message from Spirit on Behalf of Oliver

Your horse Oliver is feeling the wish to go home. He just isn't feeling well. He doesn't know why. It isn't his time, so we will see what the problem is. He says he aches all over. We can't determine anything specific. The problem with aches all over may be arthritis or rheumatism that has got him depressed. If the pain can be controlled, he will be good again. If he won't cooperate, he will not eat, be depressed, wither away. No need for this to happen yet. We will talk to him. Humans take Tylenol.   Hammel the Sun

Message from Oliver

My home here is wonderful, but I can't seem to enjoy anything. I ache all over, a tired feeling. Just don't feel like doing anything. I know I am feeling sorry for myself, but it is easier to stand still and not move. I think I am not young *anymore. This is all I know about myself. Maybe something to take this feeling away, as I do not like it. Someone is asking me to tell them where I hurt. All over! Just let me be; I am old and tired. Ache all over. Your tender care and concern upsets me that I can't tell you something I don't know.*

Oliver

Oliver was started on anti-inflammatory medicine to help with his pain. Gradually, he started to eat and gained all his weight back. There was a noticeable change in his demeanour. He once again started to be the boss man of the herd, playing with his buddies.

Years later, now 27 years of age, Oliver wanted to tell his owner more about himself and his past lives.

Oliver's Message to His Owner

I write once more as time is passing quickly and haven't told you all about myself. No one asks but I wish to tell I have always been a good animal, worked hard on a farm proved of how strong I was. Many lives before in a land, cold, ice, snow, I was a huge Stallion. I fought battles bitterly bent on killing, as this was what was expected of a lead horse to battle. Sometimes we had a banner of pride for our clan. Knives, swords, arrows were my rider's defence. No one could conquer us as we were that fierce. No mercy just kill. Not one horse or man had fear of passing over. To die in battle was an honour bequeathed in honour and glory.

When I gave up my life crossing over, I saw what a horrible horrendous life cycle it was. The ones I had held in high esteem had flattened villages with no exceptions. Other animals showed me the way, other than what I knew. I longed to makeup in the next life for what I had been part of. That was when I became a farm horse. Worked hard morning to night to supply food for this family. The plague took them suddenly, I was left alone to look after myself. Wandering around I found a farm that welcomed another horse. This life is easy now. I am left with aches and pains from other lives, but I am good.

Tilley – Big Attitude, Tiny Horse

Tilley requested to communicate herself but would not identify who she was. It was later determined that it was because she didn't like to be referenced by her name.

Like humans, animals return to new life cycles to develop their soul through life lessons on earth. In Tilley's case her lesson to be learned was humility. Proud of her stance of an Arabian horse in her past life, she displayed discontent being a miniature horse. This was demeaning to her. A very strong-willed miniature horse wanting to tell her story from a previous life.

First Message from Tilley

I was an Arabian horse, so pure, so magnificent to behold. Treasured was I by my master. I was guarded, protected, sleeping in the tent with him and his family. We were a tribe, some called Bedouins, robbing all that fell under his hands. I was agile, fast, ferocious, strong, everything needed when robbing, then a fast getaway. I was bred to a magnificent stallion, so was in foal.

We were out one night to scavenge some travellers, a perfect attack and a quick retreat, hopefully stealing whatever was available to steal. The guards caught us, and a battle, violent in nature, happened. Some were killed on both sides. I was hit with an arrow to my side.

I had to get my master back to our camp. He was not injured, but they would have killed him if I left him there unprotected. Gruelling as it was, I managed to return to the camp. The most attentive care could not heal me. I stayed barely alive to sire my small but determined stallion to birth.

My last memory was my master holding my head on his lap, telling me his love, how courageous I was. I slipped away with the memory of a beautiful, black, weak-legged foal, not aware of the sacrifices made in order to leave a heritage to carry on. I loved my master!

I was allowed to return for another life cycle. I look at myself and wonder why I chose to be what I am in this life. A raggedy miniature. I was told I needed to learn humility; I am not sure why! When I complain, I am told I chose this life. True, I am loved and cared for, but trotting around pulling a cart is just too much humility. My girl enjoys this so much that it makes up for what I have become. In her eyes, I am wonderful, so I must believe this to be so, but oh, what a different shape to contend with.

I am adjusting. When I return home, there must be a special place for me as I have learned humility abundant.

QUESTION: Why won't you sign your name?

Tilley's REPLY: *Because I do not like my name. Want a more elegant name to remind me I was a purebred Arabian horse.*

QUESTION: Are you unhappy?

Tilley's REPLY: *No, disgruntled. Can't change me back, need a nicer name as I must feel important, elegant, none of this cute stuff reminding me of how I look now. Must have been crazy to come back like this miniature. The Creator did it, not me! Not disrespectful, but I can't understand why it was my decision! I will not sign this horrible name, Tilley.*

QUESTION: Do you like any of the names picked out?

Tilley's REPLY: *I don't know yet, let me think about it.*

QUESTION: Until you decide, can we call you Tilley?

Tilley's REPLY: *No.*

QUESTION: So, what should she call you in the meantime?

Tilley's REPLY: *Call me Samara. That will be my name. I don't think I look like Samara, maybe Naila. When you call me by these two names, see which one I answer to. I will see which one I am comfortable with, just not Tilley!*

Upon research, it was determined there was, and still is, a Bedouin tribe located in the Middle East. Even though they are no longer nomadic, these tribes originally pillaged caravans in the desert to survive.

Abby – Gone but Forever Present

Abby was an Arabian horse bought by his owner as her first horse. Abby was purchased at the age of seven and passed away at twenty-one years of age. A horse nobody wanted, an owner determined to make it work. An endless relationship that is still present to this day.

Message from Abby

    This is Abby, your companion in your younger years. We grew up together. We had fun, both young with a lot to learn, some easy, some more difficult, but always special. I had Arabian blood flowing through me, so I was a bit more difficult to handle. Not everyone understood like you did, that I would never be mean or hurt anyone. This caused difficulties as I was sold many times, never to experience the special times you and I had. I was never mistreated, but also never understood. I became hard to handle until I was sold to a man who finally talked to me gently, calmed me, told me I was hot-blooded but could restrain myself. I did pass under his care (another life).

    I have never had an opportunity before to tell you how much I cared for you. You didn't always do things right. Me either, but between the two of us, we grew up together. So sad to leave you. I tried to understand why but knew if there was any other way, you would have taken another path. I wish you to know I have the most wonderful memories of our time together that I remember on this side. I watch you with your animals; many you treat as you did me. Don't forget me as I was your first love. I was blessed to be with you.

Love and Light follow you always,

Abby

Rules – A Champion Inside and Out

Rules was a quarter horse gelding who passed away in 2017 at the age of twenty-five. Rules knew his job as a show horse and excelled at it. He seemed to love his show life, but his owner wanted to know if this was indeed the case. With previous communicators, Rules always referred to himself as a champion. A writing was done, and an answer was given.

Message from Rules from the Other Side

In my Earth cycle with my mistress, I have communicated myself to others. Mistress and I knew we were meant to be together. Her goals were my goals, not only to please her but for myself. I loved the glory of winning.

One time, we won, received a trophy, then a lady came over to congratulate us on a good win. She rubbed my muzzle, talked so tenderly to me. I understood her, but she spoke different. She told me not to strain. I was using up energy to be saved for the end time. I was a beautiful horse who deserved to win. She turned to Mistress, but Mistress didn't understand her and said she didn't speak French. Before she left, she whispered in my ear we would see each other again, here or in the after. I felt a close kinship, almost much as I have with Mistress. No one can be as much to me as my mistress.

Do not be upset what was done to win. I felt the same. If you had asked my opinion, I would have told you the win was important above all else. You never did anything to hurt me that I would do for myself. Whatever we did together was special. The only time I was upset and really angry with you—when you were to sell the place. I tried to tell you, but you kept not understanding why I was so unruly, hard to handle.

Finally, you had a lady who could read me. I was able to tell her why I was upset. Then you knew my problem. You reassured me I was your special horse, never to part until it was my time to pass over. You would never sell me. Wherever you settle, there always would be a place for me. We were so compatible, loving. You talked to me, told me your problems that upset you. I was a good listener but also caring. We enjoyed the wins, the trophies. We worked together as one, a team effort. We grew up together, made mistakes, forgiving, then focused on the goal together. A wonderful life together to experience. We will *remember each other in fondness and love. Once again, to be together on this side. Our Creator has been good to us. Walk in His light.*

Rules

The owner confirmed that there was a show where a lady had approached Rules, whispered into his ear, and affectionately patted and talked to him. The owner, unable to speak French, had no idea what was said, but knew the lady was fond of the horse.

Cherokee – Happy Trails till We Meet Again

Telepathically, I kept hearing the song "Happy Trails to you, until we meet again." I was prompted to write, and to my surprise, a family horse from our younger years (the late 60s) was steadfast in giving a message. This was my oldest daughter's first horse, a palomino gelding renamed Cherokee. When my oldest daughter needed a car, Cherokee was swapped for a Volkswagen Beetle and given to my younger daughters as their first horse. Cherokee's original name was Trigger. According to my oldest daughter, Cherokee would occasionally bow and do a parade walk for no apparent reason, unknown until now.

In the writing Cherokee describes his life with his first owner. Trained to perform for an audience, it was a rewarding life. Then tragedy struck and Cherokee's owner passed away. Life for the horse took a turn for the worse as he was sold and resold. Different owners, misunderstanding the horses training. Finally, the horse was sold to a family whose demands were minimal. Once again life was good.

First Message from Trigger/Cherokee

I have lived many lives, had many names. My last life was a wonderful ending after enduring uncertainties, not physical, but just lost and not wanted. My partner and I were together from first I can remember. We were a team trained to ride together, please everyone with tricks that audiences enjoyed. A lot of attention. I was well-trained, never a spoken word as to what feat, trick we were to perform. I knew he depended on me to secure him in place when he rode me sideways, not move when he stood upon my back. I would end our concert with my bowing to the crowd. Even when getting older, we could please the crowds. This was a wonderful life we lived.

I didn't fully understand what was happening, but my beloved Boss told me he would see me on the Other Side. He told me I would be well looked after as there was money for my care till we would meet again. So sad he was gone.

I went to a stable that did look after me. He wanted to ride, but I kept responding to what I knew to be signals, sometimes roll over, prance and one where I would rear up. He sold me. Angry with me, he was hurt; I don't think badly. Just couldn't work together for his liking. I think he kept the money as I was never looked after well after that.

I was sold many times. They said I was

impossible, then would be sold again. I felt a hopeless life, longed to return home, join my Boss. Sometimes, I thought I could hear him sing to me, but that disappeared with time. I had no hope. When this young girl looked at me, it was love at first sight. She was so happy with me; thought I was handsome.

There were a few upsets with signals, but she talked to me. I tried to listen instead of responding with different pressure. Happiness was complete. There was two more to love me, ride me. I realized I had to look after them as they were so dumb, didn't know anything about horses. I was needed. I prompted them. Sometimes, I embarrassed them. They would signal me; I would bow, not at the right time. They were never angry at me; just more love, don't do that. Why do you do that?!

Time moved on; it was a long life I lived. A new horse came along, not room for two. Fear I would be sold, unrest as I was really old. I was given away where there were two other horses. We were all friends. I felt it was my duty to look after them. I had the joy of children all around me. My favourite place was where there was an apple tree. There, they finally laid me to rest. Many tears but many happy memories for all. My "T" called me Cherokee no more.

Trigger, Happy Trails.

QUESTION: Are you Roy Rogers' Trigger?

Cherokee's REPLY: *You make me laugh. Yes, I can (laugh). I am not Roy Rogers' Trigger, but I do look like him. I was chosen for this reason. I was smart, capable of doing the tricks, same as that Trigger. The difference was obvious. My Boss and I worked hard to do the tricks the other Trigger could do. I was really good, pleased with what Boss and I could do. We pleased crowds. They would get the crowds excited playing music of Roy. The ending of my bowing and the music "Happy Trails to you, until we meet again" was played.*

A glorious time for us. Boss had many girlfriends. He had a charm but not so good-looking. When he rode me, we looked really great. We were popular; it ended too soon. He took ill; no one could take over with me. I just couldn't respond to anyone else as I did to him. I lived a long life, some not so good, but a wonderful, peaceful passing. I was buried under my favourite place, the apple tree. My Boss sang to me as I passed over—our song. We did meet again. His voice was not a true singer but music to my ears. I loved those dumb horse girls. I was needed to look after them until they got their horse know-how.

The Cherokee Trigger

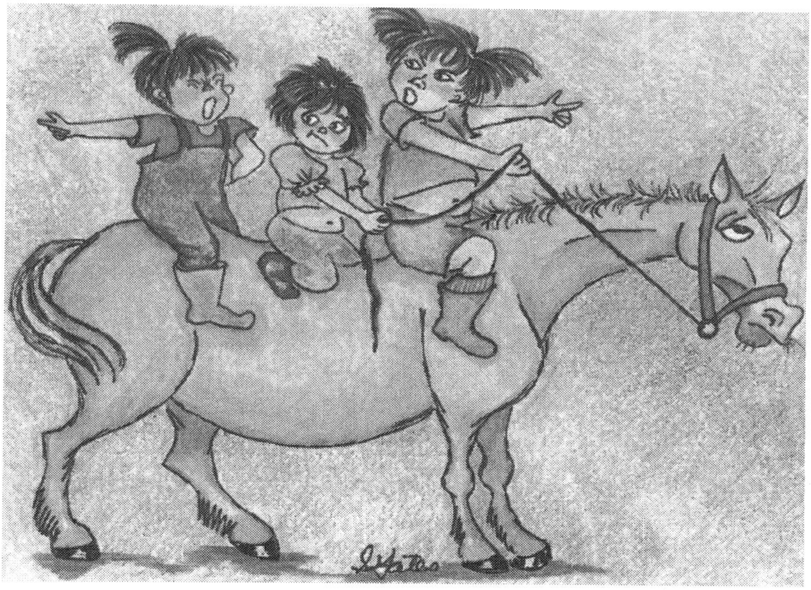

Moonie – His Memory Lives On

Moonie (Midnight Smokey Grey 919) was the first Newfoundland pony to be grandfathered into the registry. He was a history-making pony whose portfolio was the benchmark for future grandfathering. He was the heart and soul of Willow Creek Stables, a rescue for Newfoundland ponies.

Moonie fell sick and gradually stopped eating. Despite countless vet visits, they were unable to determine what was wrong. A writing for Moonie was done in the hopes of finding out more about his condition.

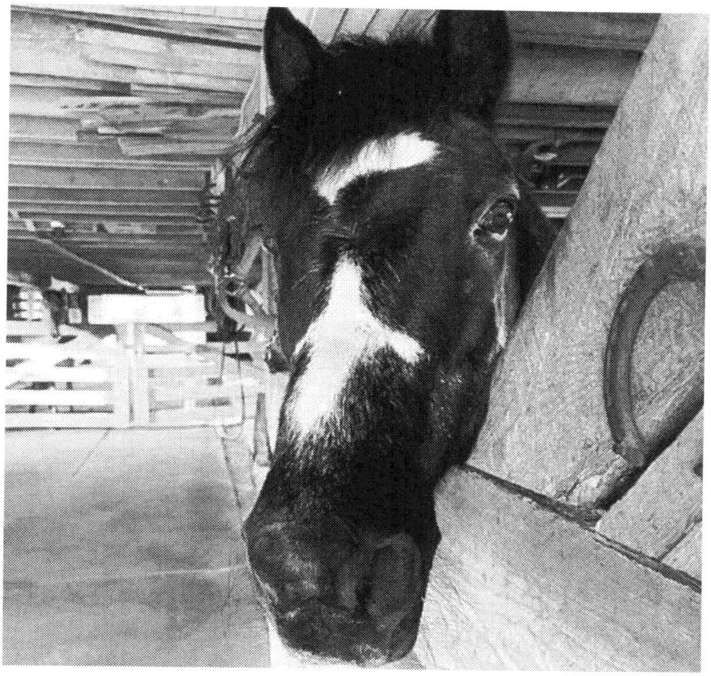

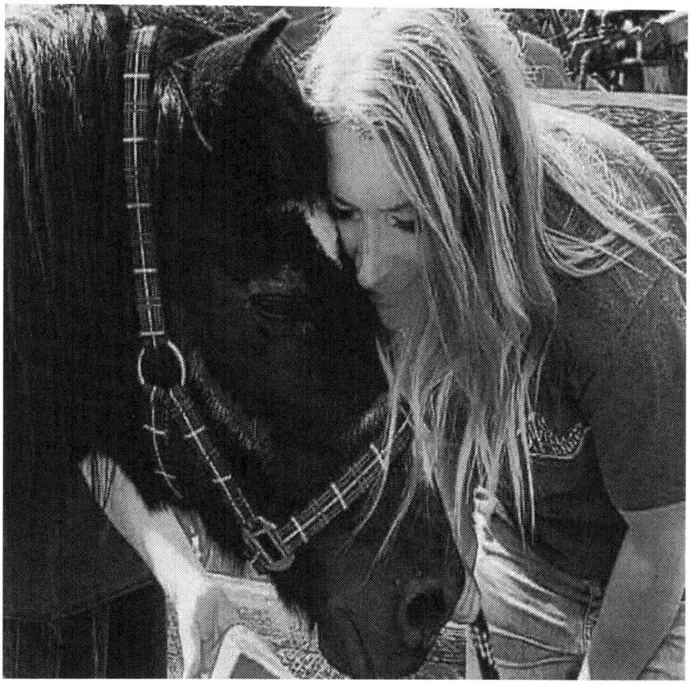

Message from Moonie

I have been loved, kindness, even talked to, always so tender, which made up for my younger years. I had fear, did not understand, felt I was not what they had wanted or expected from me.

Here, now, this has been a special person, so real in someone's life, needed, comforted for the both of us. But now it is different. I am so tired; I wish to return home to my Creator. Run in the green fields, see my friends, feel good again. I am so tired. I want you to understand me.

I once was a beautiful black steed, full of energy, prancing, pawing the ground, almost unable to wait for the moment of battle. The Colonel and I were one, a fighter, warrior with no fear, only anxious for the excitement of battle. We believed nothing could stop us as it had never happened before. We were victorious, proud in our abilities to fight, kill as many enemies that came under Colonel and his mighty sword. It happened! We were both struck down. It took two warriors to disable us, swift with swords. Two huge armies fighting, so many killed, left to die.

We, my Colonel and I, badly wounded, lay for many days to die. Together as we had lived, finally passing over together, but not in this life. I had you, quiet, stable love, understanding me as I did you.

Now it is time for me to return home to my Creator, the green pastures that I can once again run, feel the wind, free from all this tiredness, old. I have lived this good life with you, happy companions, but now let me go. This parting is sad for me, too, but it is my time. Once more, a bit of sweet oats to take me on my journey home. The sweetness will remind me of you, my dear one, good memories always. Don't forget me till we are together again.

Moonie's condition continued to deteriorate. He passed peacefully with his owner by his side. His message after passing is one of love and appreciation.

Message from Moonie to His Owner After His Passing

I longed for green pastures but was torn between staying and going. I saw you and did want to stay, all love, but it was my time. This cannot be changed. I am here; you are there. I know how close we were bonded. This will not change but carry on. There is more than one life to live. We will be together again.

What I explained to you about what I did for my master, ravaging, stealing, was a life I was so magnificent, a black stallion. My life with you this time was a pony, opposite in stature, such a change, but you loved me as I was. There is pride in what you are doing in remembrance of me. It was selfish of me, thinking only of myself, feeling sorry for myself. Felt ugly, didn't know why you cared for me. I know people suffer depression, so do animals. I was one! I don't believe I wanted to upset you; only felt sorry for myself. Selfish, maybe for attention, it matters not really. Even though it was my time to pass over, I should have showed how much I cared for you right up to the last moment.

Think positive. Know we will be together again, on this side, when you join me, maybe when we plan another life together. You do not understand. I wish to explain. All life is in cycles. Born, live, passed back over to our Creator. We must live the best we can, to others, to ourselves. Love is most important, this you and I had. Our good memories are what count now. Do not waste time in mourning, worrying if you did the right thing. There is not wrong thing! My time on Earth was finished. I knew this; that is why I was in mourning for myself. I did not want to leave but knew it would happen. I should have enjoyed this time until I was called. Now, it is time for you to stop all this fretting. Enjoy what is around you. Keep my memory alive, but not in sadness, but happy for our time together. I will be your mascot forever. Smile and be happy.

Moonie

Gimble – It's a Wonderful Life

Gimble, a Newfoundland pony, is living life to the fullest. He resides on the farm where he was born. Gimble has always been challenging, never mean, but pushing the limits in the name of fun. Recalling his horrific past life cycle, his only resolve was to live a happy life.

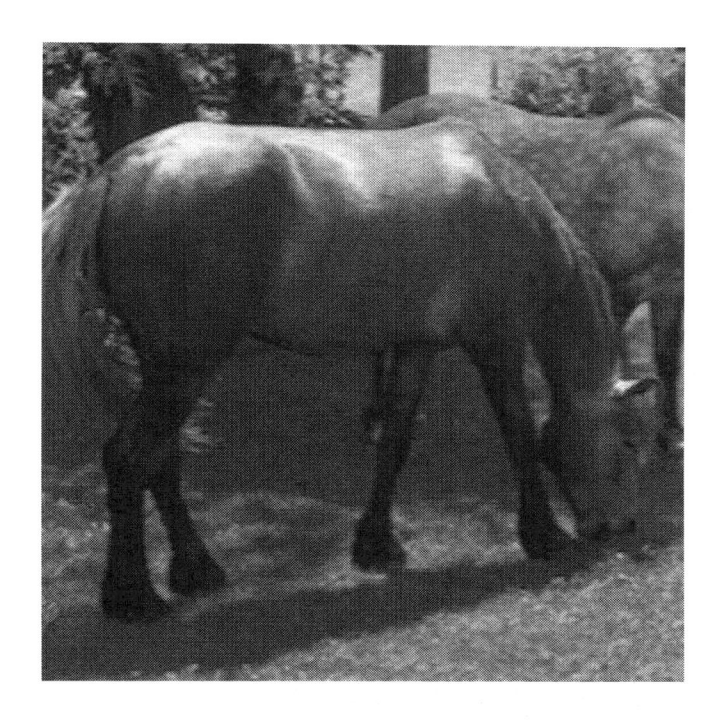

Message from Gimble

This is Gimble, as you have been told, Nella's foal. To be born into such love and care, I have no complaints. This life is full of fun. I think I am a better horse than my mom, as she has her own way. I deserve this wonderful life; accept it to the fullest. I still carry the scars of a prior life, so this life I will live to the fullest. Not mean, but my way, bossy to do my thing.

The prior life that keeps coming back to me was a long life of hardship that I had to endure. My master had a terrible temper. He took to beating me when anything displeased him, not of my doing but there to take it out on. He would be sorry, look after my cuts, as there were many. I accepted this abuse as I thought I did something wrong, submissive, accepting a future I did not understand. I was so damaged that I could not be ridden. The pain in my body was so intense this made him angrier.

Time passed blurred to me, but I knew the

beating became less. He was angry that he was weak. Didn't see him, didn't have anyone feeding me. Thought I would starve to death; then a lady came to me. She bore the scars like me. She fed me, gave me water. She told me she had no money and had to sell me. I think we cried together as we were both so damaged.

A man came to pick me up, took me away with him. I was with a herd of other horses. We travelled all together. There was food to graze on, stop at night near water. Time passed like this. Then we were at a place that was fenced in, big groups of us. Some of the better horses were taken away. I was not. What happened next put great fear in me as I could not understand. The other horses went wild trying to break out; I think corral stampeding, fear, all out of our minds not knowing, just pure panic to be free.

Some got away, others were rounded up, as me, back to the fear of the unknown. Some humans were hurt, died, non-deliberate. I am now sorry as I was a cause of one of the kindest men. Others deserved what happened to them; they were mean, whipping us. Not him. Always be sorry of how I hurt him and he passed over.

We met on the Other Side. I was forgiven by him; this was his kind nature. Now, I must forgive me. I have not met the mean man on this side or here; don't mind at all. See why I deserve this fine life now, pampered, a mama, a kind, loving family, humans, horses, dogs, animals. My over there is here. Yes, I am surrounded by love, also returned. Gimble.

Nella – A Word from the Wise

Nella, a Newfoundland pony was purchased by her current owner as a green riding prospect. When Nella was sent to be trained to pull a cart. She took to it like she had been trained in the past. However, as the training commenced, Nella began to bolt for no apparent reason, becoming very dangerous. Nella writes about the relationship between human and horse. She recalls a passed life pulling a chariot, but had no desire to pull a cart in this life cycle. In the interim, Nella and her owner are enjoying time out on the trails.

Message from Nella

You are told I am Gimble's Mama. That is right for this life. Humans and animals come back many times, many lives, all animals for the love of man. Kindness, love, brings out the best in both. Things go astray when the chosen path is ignored. Man has free will. Animals, not so much. Animals depend on man, mostly to set them on their path, right or wrong, depends on respect, love shown to the animal. No human or animal comes to Earth life perfect. How you pass over—a better soul—is what is important. Somehow, this is a challenging time forgotten by most all. I am a horse. I know better, but still do my own thing. Discipline, teaching animals how to behave is not wrong, especially with love.

I disappointed my mistress because I didn't want to be chained to a cart. Maybe I felt I was too good for this type of thing. It was below me. I will tell you why!

I was a handsome, large horse bred to chariot race. I was born a mare, very disappointing to my master. Secretly, he trained me. I was smart, obedient, all he wanted except I was not a stallion.

A vicious war broke out. He trusted me the most to take him into battle; my honour to be chosen. I did not disappoint him; was able to save him, but not myself. A cart is not a chariot, in time, maybe. My story, my mistress. Still love me.

Molson – Simple Lives

Molson's mother, a Haflinger, was rescued from a breeding farm whose sole purpose was to produce livestock for the Japanese meat market. The broodmares who could no longer produce, as well as the colts were shipped for meat while the fillies were replacements for the breeding program. Some of the herd was rescued, and many of the foals were born in the safety of a farm. The mares and foals were then found loving homes. Molson was one of those foals.

Message Received from Molson

They call me Molson. I heard them say I was rescued; I don't know what it means. I know I am happy. Many other horse friends, many dogs. I think I look different than the others, but I am treated with the same love, kindness. Almost like when I sleep, I remember another time.

I was like a donkey. I had casquets hung on either side of me; there was a cart behind me attached. We wandered alone, going from town to town, farms along the way. Times, we had little to eat, but we always found water, some farmer willing to feed us. I longed to stay when we stopped and not keep going.

There was no home for us. My man was tired. We stopped earlier than usual. He wasn't able to make a fire and said he just wanted to rest. He never moved after that. I stayed with him, hoping he would wake up. I don't know if he planned it, but we were in a beautiful knoll, water and grass.

I was looked after, but I couldn't look after him. Animals do cry. I cried. A cowboy with a herd of cattle eventually came to where I was. He dug for a place to lay my man. I joined. I looked after his cattle, alerting him if there was danger to them. I finally belonged somewhere. Missed man, then saw him when I joined my Creator. I had a happy life, always needed.

Different life this time but happy.

Your Molson, my Lady.

Paige – Things That Go Yelp in the Night

Paige's new owner requested a writing to try to find out why Paige was insistent on staying in her stall. Other questions were asked, but Paige's main focus was to let her owner understand why she was not interested in going outside.

Message from Paige

Owner's QUESTION: How old are you, and why are you unable to gain weight?

Paige's REPLY: *Why am I asked for things I don't know? How would I know how old I am? Why do I care about my weight? Really, I am a horse. I am old enough to know what I like that I can tell you.*

The barn makes me feel protected, no harm to me. Field has bad memories. I would be left out in the field; it seemed like a long time. Darkness at night scared me. I could hear yelping. I felt all alone, nothing, no one to protect me. When I was finally put back in the barn, I did not want to leave. I am not a brave horse. I need to know if I am let out, I can be assured I will be in each night. I like green grass but still have to know I can come in, go out; that is there for me.

You ask what type of riding I did. Why? I had a saddle, walked around. It was like a learning lesson, not for me but the person on my back. If I went too fast, they panicked. We just couldn't seem to connect.

I feel better where I am now; I feel really cared for. We will get along; just need a bit of time to know each other. You can ride me; just don't be afraid of me. That hurts my feelings. I want to be trusted, so I can trust you to leave the barn door always open so I can come in and go out to get my courage back. Nighttime scares me if I am left in the field.

Yes, we will be friends, pals, you will see. I like my name, Paige.

Paige had been bought at auction by her previous owner and then spent approximately eight years outside in a field—24/7—with cows. She had minimal human contact and had no other companion horses until she was purchased by her current owner.

A nutritionist and many vet calls all proved futile. Paige continued to lose weight, her condition deteriorated despite her owner's efforts.

Paige quietly passed away, and a writing was done to help provide closure.

<u>Message from Paige from the Other Side</u>

Now I know why you were concerned about my weight. I am just a horse. I blamed everything on my fears of being left out in a field. I do not know if I lose weight; this did not worry me, nor my mouth. You had a decision to decide my future. I did not know the difference between fear and pain.

Now that I am on this side, I care for you even more. We will be together again, your loving horses and you. The passing to this side is never fearful as it is for humans. We know what to expect; everything—only good. Do not ever

change your loving nature. A difficult decision for you to make but the right one, a sacrifice for you thinking only for me.
Paige

Zeta Sunni – Double the Love

Zeta was rescued from a bad situation, injured while in foal. The owner later moved away and gave Zeta to another who had been riding her for years. This woman owned Zeta for over 15 years until her passing. During that time, Zeta gave birth to a filly called Sunni.

In her senior years, Zeta developed Cushing's disease and become extremely arthritic. When Zeta's condition began to deteriorate, a connection was made to determine her state of mind and if she was ready to return to the other side. Zeta was sad to leave the one she loved but was tired and ready to go. A message from spirit consoles the owner, revealing they had many lives together and would meet again.

Final Message from Zeta

More times have we had to part only to be united on the Other Side. I have no regrets in this life as I spent this time with you. Sad I am to leave you, but my time has come. Look at my baby, and you will see me. I will go peacefully. Your love with me always. It is best now as I am tired. Even with your tender care, the time has come as I have become weary, tired, anxious to go home, sad to leave you, but the time has come.

Your pal, your friend, your companion. Our Creator's light shine upon you.

Horse Hairs Zeta

Message of Support from Spirit Concerning Zeta and Her Owner

We feel the depth of sadness in her heart for her horse. Animals can be pure joy; do not want anything but love and kindness. This has been supplied abundantly. Special are all the Blessings from above. Two-fold is the bonding for both. Zeta's name on this side is Sun Dance. They have shared lifetimes before. Also, this is where the name Sonny for her foal was prompted. The love she has for these two horses is natural and returned as it is their nature. Reassured that this bond will never be broken

Message from Zeta after Her Passing

I can't explain exactly how this happens, but with all my being that God has granted me, I can express my thoughts, love to my protector, Mistress. Do not grieve for me as I am in a place of love, like what you bestowed on me while on Earth. When you join me, eventually, we will ride like the wind, so beautiful in mind, body and soul, beyond what you could imagine.

Your Hairy Horse Zeta

In the messages, Zeta had referenced herself as Hairy Horse. Zeta had developed Cushing's disease in the latter years of her life. Because of this, Zeta had to be shaved multiple times over the summer.

Sunni was Zeta's foal and belonged to the same owner her entire life. The human-animal bond that existed between Sunni and her owner was exceptional. Sunni's first writing tells of her past life and how it influenced her to a state of anxiousness when being confined to a stall. Sunni then recalls a second past life, hard, but fulfilling as a plough horse.

When a strong bond is established, it always remains from one lifetime to the next, it is never-ending. Each life is influenced by previous life lessons learned, and emotional ties.

Message from Sunni

I forgot my symbol, but "T" will know it is me, maybe a bucket, as I like my oats. I will explain myself and why I must feel for sure that there is hay grass always there for me. Another life cycle I ran with a beautiful herd of horses. Free-spirited, running in a beautiful, plentiful valley.

Our Creator was so generous, allowing us to multiply with many foals. He blessed me with the most magnificent little black stallion, a bond of love so strong. The stallion who sired him was the accepted leader; harmony existed all around.

Then the rain didn't fall, the grass became dry, and food was not available. There was no strict rule, but we knew that grass and water must be available to the strongest to not let our herd die but to carry on. No one told us who would have to wander quietly away to pass over due to starvation. It was just taken for granted what must be done.

I slipped away to die; it is difficult to deny yourself life so that starvation would take place, but it was for the good. No fear existed to return to our Creator. Survival was something we had within us, so it was a difficult thing to do. I quietly disappeared into a treed place, laid down, trying to fight the strong urge to fight for me. Son followed me, would not leave. Stood over me, then laid down beside me. The rains came, but too late for me. Son survived to become the Lead Stallion—my pride, stamina and strength.

Now you know why I am as I am. I must see my next oats, hay available to me. Locked in a stall, not sure when I would eat again, scares me. I would be happy with grass, but if in a stall, I can only worry. I tried to tell you my worries, acted up a bit in panic, but I would never hurt you. That you know. We are bonded. You looked after me so tenderly. How could we be otherwise? You call me Sunni, but I like to remember my son as Sonny. I decided I would be your sunshine, so now you know the story.

I am so content where I am. My greatest worry is not there. I wish to stay as healthy, strong as our Creator allows me. When it is time for my calling, I will part with sadness. I will never forget our memories. You will not either. I thank my Creator for us and ask to let me stay a long time yet. He has been gracious to me and you for our binding friendship. I think this happiness has been granted to us for sacrifices we have made in prior lives. We must accept with loving thanks this special gift. Now you know me even better. My son, Sonny or the sun upon us lighting the way, it matters not. My courageous "T" friend. I like buckets full.

Sunny, both, all names

<u>Message from Sunni Height of Sickness</u>

My dearest soul, so close to me; we know each other so well. We have been through our tough times in this life, mostly sickness now, but always with enduring love for each other. We are not meant to be perfect in this life, but I believe our devotion is. I can't tell you if I will recover, but this is true; I will fight for life to be with you. The most fear I have is fire. Know I would run through fire to be with you. I have acquired strength, tolerance, determination, with love always there.

I wish to tell you why I am like I am. In another time, I was a plough horse. We worked together, my owner and I. I heard it was pioneer times. The days were long and hard, but he and I worked the fields. I knew that I was so important to him and his family. No day, no matter how tired we were, he would put his arm over me and thank our Maker, then he would thank me for a good day's work, calling me his friend.

It seemed we were together a long time but not long enough for me and him. I started to stumble; no matter how much determination I had to carry on, I fell. He held my head on his lap, crying and patting my head; no anger, just love. He told me many things, but the last was that it was time for me to go to the green field of grass and clover with his blessings. The hard times were behind us. This life with you was meant to be—a life beyond belief. You, T, "S," have given me so much love I would do anything for you.

I am determined to stay as long as I am permitted. I think running through fire must be easier than what I tolerate now. Within feels like a fire burning. I want to run away or fight those needles, but I stay as calm as I can as I know your love is there. You would not want to hurt me if there wasn't another way. Yes, I will have another day to enjoy the gifts my Maker has allowed me to experience. I have never wanted to cause tears and upsets, but am not sure why it happens.

We will enjoy new tricks that you can think up for me. I will tease you to keep your attention, pretending I don't always understand. Our game—just you and me together. I love your *children, the little one just wanting to be like Grandma, "S" in between enjoying both. Worry not about our parting time. Let's enjoy each day provided to us by our Maker, love and be loved. All will be as it will be. Different spelling matters little as long as it sounds like Sonny.*

Know what is written as true.

Our Creator's Blessing Always.

Sunni eventually recovered from her sickness. She was moved to a larger stall with a window to the inside of the barn where she presently enjoys watching the human/horse activity. Her stall also butts up to the indoor outhouse, where she happily greets the users.

Third Message from Sunni

This is your devoted Sonny, Sunni; you know me, whatever my name is spelled, funny to me as I am the same, answers to all. I think a bucket, but again, you know me. I must tell you, my Lady "T", I am old. My bones, all of me, should have passed over. There are green pastures, no pain over there but, I will stay as long as I can. Your loving care has held me on to you but know God's Will will never separate us. You need me as I have needed you, it will and always been like this. I have never been a perfect horse, but in your eyes, I could do no wrong. In my eyes, you are perfect, loving, caring for me.

I have caused you many times pain, injury that I never wanted to happen. With all my dwindling strength, I did not roll over as what should have been. The pain, my weak bones, just gave out. The many ties you have tended to me, not allowing me to leave, are within me, always in my heart. I will stay with you as long as my Creator allows me to. I will endure every pain just to be with you a minute longer. Know our future is beautiful together, bonded as we are.

There are many on the Other Side loving you as they also received your loving care. After I leave, you will have another one for your care, but you must watch your health as you have and are doing so for me. I am anxious to see the one of "S's". I hope I will be there for her also. You have brought the love and respect for animals to your offspring. Our Creator looks upon you with joy. The offsprings taught to enjoy me; I them. "M," (grandchild) so determined to please herself and me. "S" so much like you, so much love and respect. I say to you, my "T", you have given me so much in this life cycle. I wish I could have given you more, less hurt; this is my regret. I wish to see my "S's" offspring with joy.

My loving Blessings always,

Sonny/Sunni

Hitch – A Hero of His Own Story

Hitch was a three-year-old quarter horse when the accident occurred. While at a show, the rider was exercising Hitch, and a storm came out of nowhere. As the rider was ready to dismount, a violent, clash of thunder caused the horse to bolt out of fear. The rider ended up underneath the horse and was thrown between two steel bars. The injuries were so severe for the rider that a full body scan was taken, and a brain tumour was discovered. Events leading up to the accident seemed to be so synchronized that there was no question that this was fate.

Message from Hitch

You know me as Hitch. I was steady, easy to ride and loved. What changed all this was not my fault but meant to be—the Creator's bidding to save one of His Earth Angels. I had to sacrifice myself at His bidding. I willingly did so, not exactly sure how this was to happen. It was unexpected; I didn't have to think what was happening.

There was a storm, not terrible, but all of a sudden, lightning, then a crash of thunder. I bolted, scared out of my mind, threw my rider off. She fell. Hit her head hard. I was so upset, but there was nothing I could do. I watched, I cried, felt scared, so scared she was badly hurt. I thought I was to protect her. Look what I did; shame was mine. Tears were all around me. The blame was mine. She was taken to the hospital. Such a commotion, but no one thought to say right away it was not my fault. I suffered, so blamed myself.

Finally listening, I heard said she had a tumour. The fall had revealed this, that it was in her head. She recovered, but they had lost their trust in me. I know that was why I was given away. Nothing I did was good; listening did not change this fate. I was cared for by my new girl, but the scar was within me, never to leave me. I tried to please my new owner, but it didn't work out. In my trying to please her, I seemed to do everything wrong. I became a useless horse. Even though the accident was meant to be and saved the Earth Angel of our Creator, I could not forgive myself. I should have been able to have controlled myself better. Even on this side, knowing the reason, but still sad.   Hitch

Animals have many roles to play on this side and the Other Side of the veil. Sometimes, it is to teach love and empathy. However, in Hitch's case, he was a major catalyst for an event that was destined to happen.

Georgia – A Word of Advice

Georgia, a quarter horse mare, was given to a family who had just lost their horse. They loved and cared for Georgia until her passing. Georgia writes to her previous owner about her confusion of being relocated to a new home without explanation. She emphasizes a message that would benefit all animal owners; talk to your animals; they understand.

Georgia then goes on to explain a past life where she was ruthlessly mutilated in a dispute between two tribes. Animals like humans undergo both good and bad lives so they can relate and aid in the healing of those who experience trauma in their life here on earth.

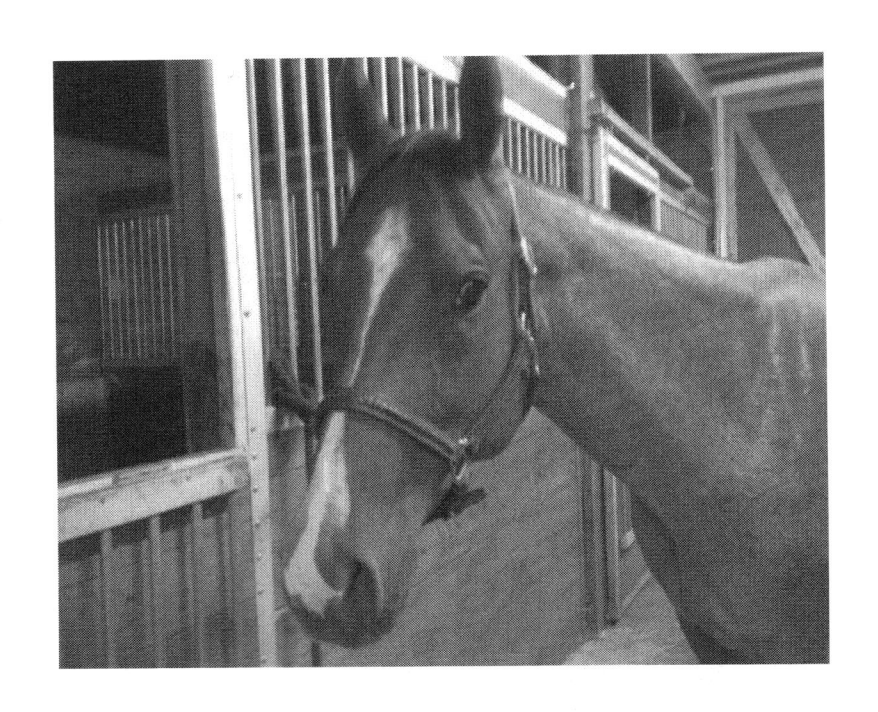

Message from Georgia from the Other Side

You ask of me, the one Georgia—always said to be a good girl. Why, then, get rid of me? I did go to a good person, but still, you didn't talk to me or tell me. This is difficult just being with you, then off somewhere else to stay. You should have told me, explained. I heard you tell it was to a girl who had just lost her horse. Why not say so? I tell you this as on this side we wish to make amends you, me. Don't do this again; even if reason is good, don't do it; explain. If I had to go to someone else, then it could not have been a better place. I needed security. My life cycle was wonderful, full of love, kindness. On this side, I realize so much what good souls are on Earth. Many animals pass over in pure horror as to how they have been mistreated.

We all work together to restore their beautiful souls that have been so badly damaged. Humans, animals go through life cycles that are both good and bad. This way, we know how it feels to be mistreated, which allows us to understand to help others. I do not wish to remember, but you, I will tell.

The Earth where I was had untold prosecutions, meanness unnecessary. There was only an elite that ruled. Punishment was an enjoyment, brutal in all forms, sometimes against each other, a game for enjoyment. I was owned by such one. Beautiful, a pride to behold to all who saw me.

A dispute broke out among themselves.

Vindictiveness raged in anger and malice. No one human or animal could be saved. I was stolen for the purpose to punish my master. I was mutilated beyond human decency, then dumped in front of my master's domain. Suffering, wishing to pass over, left enough alive to make my master end my life humanely. The cruelty had to end. An uprising took place. All were desecrated. Peace after a bloody battle ending such untold tyranny. This untold story happened in the tribes of the desert, now long forgotten.

This tale to be told by Georgia.

Reggie – A Transformation

Reggie was acquired by a rescue, his history unknown. In his writing, he tells of his past. The photos below show his condition when he first arrived at his new home, then six months later after some much-needed TLC.

In Reggie's message he explains what he experienced after his owner passed away. The sacrifice that his mother made to save him when the situation seemed dire. He explains how he survived until he was rescued. A heartwarming story as told by a feral horse.

Message from Reggie

They call me Reggie. Why, I am not sure, but it is fine with me as I don't remember another name. I was happy, birthed by one I called Mum. This gentle, kind man made sure we were well looked after, food, but Mum said love. He would put his head next to her, words were said. I don't know what. He came less and less to see us.

The last I remember him, he was stumbling, walked with a stick. Whispering to her, I could only hear him say someone will look after you and baby. Tears flowed from both of them. I did not know why then. He had made sure there was water and plentiful food to last long.

Mum looked after me, wanted me strong and healthy. I didn't miss him like she did. Cold came, but no one else to look after us. She showed me how to eat the white stuff for water. Bad animals were all around. Mum said they just needed food.

She laid down more often until she did not get up anymore. Nothing I did would make her move or get up. The animals broke in. I hid, as when I saw what they did to her, tearing into her body. I hid. She had told me when green appeared, I was to leave. Do not stay. I now know she gave her life for me. As long as the animals had her for food, they would not need me.

Green began to appear. I found I could eat it. Each light, I would go a little further. I began to not return back as Mum... was hard to see what *they did to her. She visited me, made me leave all behind. She told me she was in a wonderful place the Creator had for all. It was not my time to join her, so I must carry on without her. She knew that there was a plan for me. Green was not as much as before, water also. Rain came down, then I was able to carry on. I could hear Mum say, just wait, good things are to happen to you, just hold on!*

I only knew one human, had difficulty knowing words like Mum and him. I was terrified as humans were all around me. When their hands reached for me, I was sure it was to tear my body like happened to Mum. I don't know what happened; I only remember their hands patted me gently. I just gave up. It felt like Mums gentle near. My mind came back to me. They were kind to me. Explained to me they were not all my Mums. Each had their own names. They said the word all had been rescued. I was not different; looked a lot worse than them. I showed from the outside, but many of them hurt from inside. I was easier to heal. I learned words. Brush meant that good feeling on my body. Oats, yes. The words that seemed to make me feel good inside were, "Trust me, I won't hurt you." "I will look after you."

Mum said where she was was beautiful; it could not be better than where I am.　A thank you, Reggie

Shanna, Mishka, Patti – A Story of Three

Shanna was acquired as a foal from a urine farm. When Shanna was asked to tell us about the conditions of the farm, the writing got scrambled. As explained in a later writing to the communicator, three different horses all related to the same owner wanted to tell their story at the same time.

Sometimes, connecting telepathically with one animal can be intercepted by another who wishes to speak. Communication was then divided among the three horses. Shanna is the foal purchased by the owner, the broodmare is Shanna's mother, and Patti is another horse purchased by the owner.

Shanna begins the communication talking about her life with her owner. A wonderful life full of love. She mentions the horse called Patti who was bought then later sold as she was uncontrollable and damaged due to her abuse from a former owner.

The next writing was Shanna's mother, Mishka, a

broodmare on a urine farm. She explains her life of producing one foal after another, the disappointment when they were taken away. She then tells of her previous life, and why she chose this life on a urine farm.

The final message is from an Arabian horse named Patti. Pattie was purchased by the same owner who owned Shanna. Shanna's owner understood the cruelty and abuse which Patti endured throughout her life. Hopeful that providing Patti with a loving home, Patti would once again begin to trust. This was not the case. Patti's behavior remained uncontrollable and dangerous, lashing out every chance she got. The owner finally surrendered Patti to a professional who dealt with damaged animals.

Message from Shanna

I wish to explain what happened in that foolish writing. My broodmare from the urine farm wanted to tell her story. Another, always mean horse, wanted to write her story. I tried to tell mine, but I am a polite one, so just gave up. We each will tell ours separately.

I was with my Mom in the field. I wanted tenderness from her, but she would push me away. It looked like sadness in her eyes, gentle but sad.

There were people looking at us from a little ways away. I did not know words yet, just a few when man came around. One kept looking at me, I liked her. She coaxed me to let her near. Finally, maybe curiosity, I let her near. I had to leave Mom to be with her. This was difficult to be torn away from all I knew. I did not know words. I was really scared. I was in a barn, a stall, never knew anything like this. There was never anyone that told me why I kept being in a different place. Living was good, but didn't understand that I was in foal, new word to me.

When I foaled, there was this funny-looking, tiny horse. My whole heart poured out to him, my little stallion, they said. There was so much concern, confusion, as it outside, was turning cold. Words said worry; it seemed he may be too young to survive. I never experienced a horse so full of energy, jumping around, into trouble; just terrible. I could not believe he came out of me. They said it was time to geld him. Not known to me this word. Whatever it was, it sure slowed him down. My girl loved us both.

Why she sold him, I could not understand. I now knew and felt why my mother was so distant, as she knew we would be separated. Many times, going through this heartache was her life. I was smart, obedient, always told I was beautiful, loved. I was taken to show me off. When others agreed, I had a ribbon. This made My girl happy, so I was happy. Each time I was moved to another place, it brought me closer to her.

I was first in a barn where I didn't seem to see anyone too much. I remember it was My girl's barn. Head's barn, then a wonderful, happy My girl's place. I enjoyed each place differently as I did not know differently. Dad made a garage into two stalls, my girl close by in her house. It would have been glorious except for a crazy horse (Patti) in the next stall. Never forget her name; don't even want to think about her, so miserable. They said she was like that as she had been abused. Finally sold, good riddance.

I was so happy, well-fed, trouble getting through the backdoor, not in foal, just a weight problem. People stopped by, fed me carrots. I had a large pasture, everything was good.

Time to move again. I was really upset. Really, no explanation; just loaded up, time to go. I didn't want to. First, I thought it was for a show. I was excited; this didn't happen. Oh, I was so unhappy. My girl was with me, so I didn't think I was sold.

Each move got better. This last one was my resting place. Very, very old, but a happy life to leave. I am now on this side; sorry to leave my girl, but we both have good memories, good times.

I was liked by many people, but my girl was my only special one. I now know why Patti was like she was. I now know the abuse she endured, others also. I am sorry I was always angry with her; she is my friend here. I can now show her love and kindness. Our Creator shows us the way also.

My girl's Shanna

Message from Shanna's Mother, a Broodmare from the Urine Farm

I am Mishka from before. This life, I am no name that they call me that I know. I am used for urine. Like many others here, just one of many. A broodmare that is always putting forth new foals. I know no other way in this life.

My firstborn I thought I was meant to keep by my side for always, but it was taken away. Each time I foaled, there was only a short time together. So many times of happening made me try not to hope that I could keep one. I know not how many. I heard talk, the one here, that one there. I knew large bunches were sold, had to be fat as they were to be for meat. A few were kept to become new broodmares as needed for replacing old ones or other problems.

I wish you to know about a happy time for me, maybe the only time. My beautiful baby foal that I tried so hard not to love. She was young, wanted to be loved, nurtured. I refused as I could not take another disappointment, her taken from me. We were grazing in a field; girls, sisters came over. I shied away, but they won my foal over. I was happy as she was sold to someone who would care for my little foal. I could see love there, which I had not known. Her name Shanna. This I know from this side.

Now, I wish to tell my prior life and why I chose to be born to a urine farm. A lifetime before this I was a prized mare part of a stable of the finest breed of horses, bred for endurance, good form, specific for the highest known quality. The Count sought to be known for this highest quality known. They were chosen, named from the area, country gaining great fame.

I was the prestigious result of many different

breedings to accomplish the final perfection. I know my name as it is beautiful. Mishka, the golden horse. My life cycle was not sought after ribbons but the most prestigious named horse breed winning fame. The Count sought this till meticulously he had accomplished what he believed was perfection. I chose my next life cycle to be humble, controlled, monotonous routine, no fame but worthy. My urine used for medication saves lives. I do this with pride, able to give what is needed by so many humans.

A gift from our Creator,

Mishka

Message from Patti

    My name is Patti. I write because I am sorry to those who showed me kindness and love. Meanness from my prior owner caused me to be mean, unable to accept kindness and love, to lash out to anyone, good or bad. I was controlled by horrible things that hurt. This was not needed as I was anxious to please. I knew I was hard to handle, but never would want to hurt anyone.

He did not have to twist my ears to obey. He did things to hurt me because he enjoyed it. When I was sold, I was not afraid anymore, but anger was all I knew, maybe revenge to all. Something would all of a sudden happen; my mind felt like it exploded. I was so vicious, lashing out at everything around, wanting to stamp my hooves to destroy all that hurt me, to hurt others. I had no control not to do this. I hated myself and all around me.

On this side, I feel sorrow. I was too damaged to accept the helping, loving hands extended to me. I was beyond healing. Had to return to my Creator for the healing I so badly needed. I will remain on this side until I can find the Gift of Forgiveness inside me. The sorrow of the horror of trying to hurt the one that loved me and kept trying to change my attitude will be with me. My Creator forgives me, but I can't forgive me. The one I hurt forgives me, that I am thankful for as she knows the horror I endured. Thank you.

Patti

Tyson – A Rodeo Horse's Story

Tyson was a trained bucking horse rescued at auction. When he first arrived at the farm he was terrified of humans. Horses act out on a fight or flight instinct. Tyson was a fighter. Tyson's journey to accept humans was one that required patience, love and understanding. Horses are not born with distrust and fear of all humans, it is their experience with humans that create this. It takes time for an animal who has been cruelly mistreated to learn to trust again. Fortunately for Tyson he had a soft landing with experienced caretakers who would not give up on him. Tyson's story is a story of hope for all those animals who have been rejected, abandoned, and allegedly labelled as unredeemable. Not much was known about his history, what his life was like, until now.

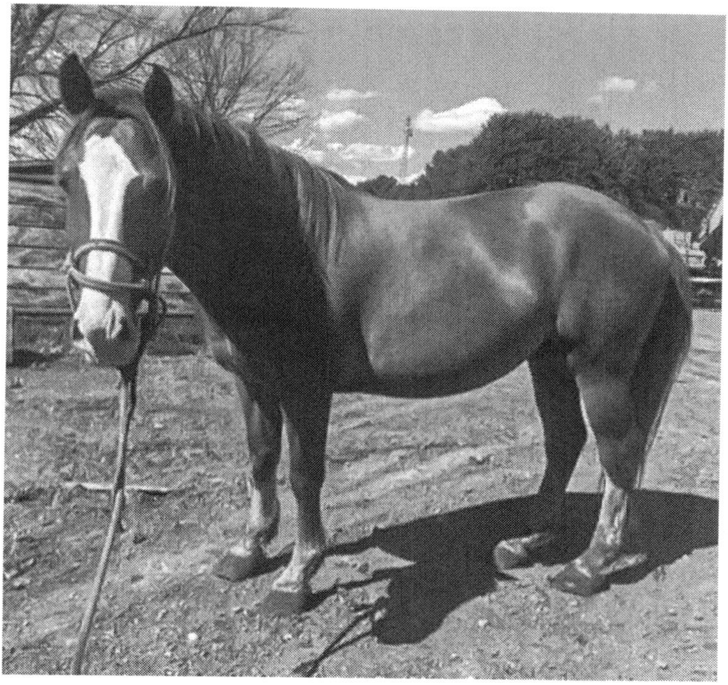

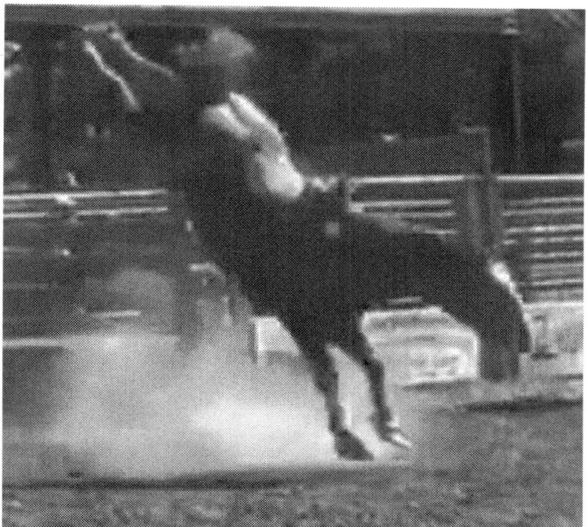

Message from Tyson

Do not judge me. I am a horse like no other, not that I want to be different. I panic easily and lash out at anything in my way. I am full of anger. Sometimes, I am out of control, a frenzy of emotions I cannot control. My mind boxes, making me crazy. I feel when I let loose then, I will feel better, but it doesn't help. I feel like there is two of me. One learning to trust, find a gentle me wanting to please. Another one that lets loose out of control, the urge to kill anything in my way. I don't want to be like this. I don't know if there is hope for me. I do not remember any peace within me.

They called me that mean horse. Watch out. I just kept getting worse. No one wanted to come near me. This only made me meaner. I just hate everyone, everything. You ask me if I am shown kindness and hope would I change. Can I trust humans? Have I ever trusted anyone in this life cycle?

When I was young, I do remember a peaceful time once. Then, the boy and I were learning to ride together. He wanted me to gallop faster and faster. I stumbled, threw him, falling on him. He didn't get up. His father came running, crying, as he couldn't bring his son back. He turned on me, so angry. I couldn't explain what had happened. I couldn't defend myself. They tried to beat me to death, many of them. They left me for dead. I wanted to return home, hurt, sick, but couldn't, knowing I had caused such a calamity of hate. I hated myself more than they did to have killed his son. It didn't matter if it was an accident. I hated myself, would not allow any kindness from anyone.

When I recovered from that beating, I was never the same, inside and out. I feel slowly a relaxing within. Whether this kindness can melt away at my meanness, I don't know. If anyone could, then it would be her. No one has ever cared for me like this. I will try. I was called the crazy mean horse.

I like Tyson; yes, I do.

Second Message from Tyson in Response to a Question about His Rodeo Days

You ask why I didn't tell you about how I was trained for rodeo. No one wanted me when I recovered. I seemed to be sold many times. My anger, hate only grew each time. I acted out, wanted to stomp, whatever I felt to do. I liked the power of fear I saw in their eyes. I was surprised when this man was pleased with my stomping, carrying on. He said exactly what he was looking for. He used me, trained me, making me even worse. I was their best show horse rearing, trying to throw the rider off. No one could remain on my back long before I threw them. This made my owners happy.

I was breaking down. They seemed to give

me stuff that made me even more crazy. It happened again, I backed up to throw myself up, felt my back legs give out. My rider was tossed, as usual, but I fell on him. Again, as before, he did not move. I really didn't care. The pain in my back legs made me lash out at everything, everyone. Many men had to give me a needle before I gave up. I had been given those needles when I was locked in a little place before performing, going out in the arena. Made me worse—crazy, strong. I was no good to them now.

I couldn't buck or throw someone off my back when standing on my back legs. I don't know what I am good for now. When I rear back, it makes me feel what I know, what I was trained for.

Never that I know, can I remember this care. Someone trying to look after me. I am afraid to let go. I am not sure what I am like inside without what I was trained for. I don't know me, myself. Can I control the urge to buck and rear?

This is the only thing I know. Who would want me? Who would trust me when I don't know myself? Something snaps in my head; I go crazy. I would have been able to accept this kindness that I now have when, before, I was just mean. That was lack of attention and jealousy as all other horses knew how to behave, commands no one bothered to care or train me. I know I am changing, a little feeling of hope. This is my last chance; I want to be able to take it. I don't like to remember, forget this. So many I caused hurt, injury. Understand.

Ebony - An Auction Horse

Unnamed was a two-year-old purchased from auction. Ebony had a great distrust and was fearful of humans. When Ebony panicked, he would lash out uncontrollably, a danger to himself and those around him. Ebony writes about his current feelings and why he chose this life cycle. He explains his past life of abuse and how he thought he had overcome his fears, however his current life experiences amplified his distrustful feelings as the horror of the past returned.

It was later confirmed that at three years of age Ebony had been sold twice at auction before he was purchased by his current owner. Ebony's second owner had forcibly trained him to ride and drive within a week using harsh methods to make him comply. A severe bit had left sores around the outside of his mouth, the damage on the inside his mouth was undeterminable.

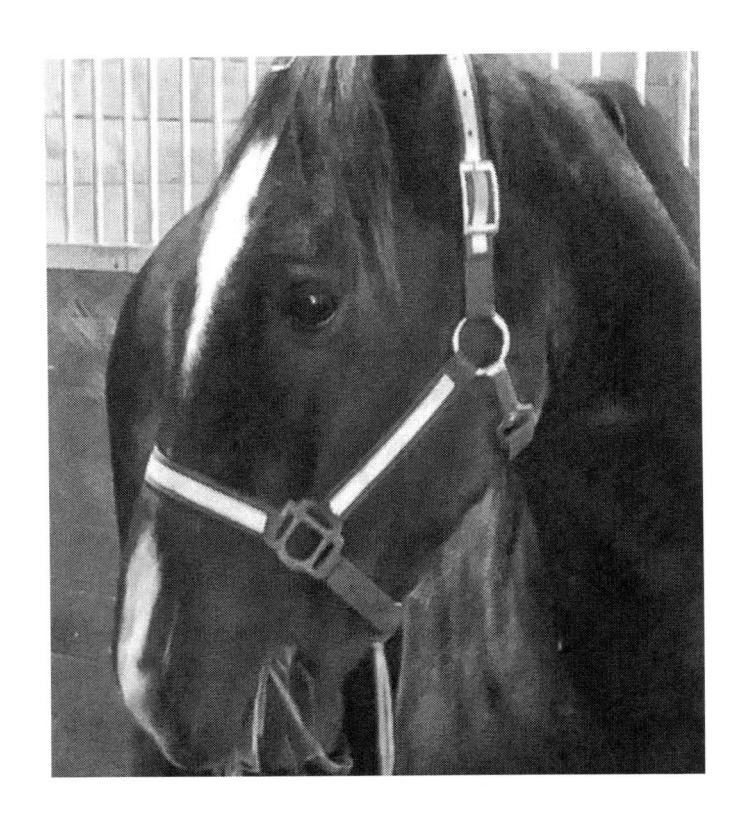

First Message from Unnamed Horse (Ebony)

I am the unnamed horse this girl bought. I know very little words. Commands, but with little understanding as to what they wanted of me. They said get rid of him, he will take too much time to train, a money loss. I was uneasy, unhappy, as I did not know what 'sold' was. It was a scary word to me. I think they said I was to be herded with the other horses.

We were all scared, uneasy as to what was to happen to us herded. Nothing bad seemed to happen. We were pushed around, did not understand. I was brought out from the others. Many looked at me, sounds were strange. This girl person looked at me kindly. I am with her now. I wonder if I train good with her. Have a name (Ebony). Still scared.

Ebony explains how he had chosen to return in this life to the same owner he had in his last life cycle as a mare.

Second Message from Ebony

I am Ebony, the second time around. I am here for you again to undo, make up, as to horrible mean horse I was. Yes, I was. I have heard you many times refer to me like that. I did deserve it. Mean, not able to accept kindness and love. I didn't hate you or want to kill you. I was just so angry, upset within. I didn't know how to change. I was not healed enough, but I was anxious to return to another life cycle to prove I was. Hatred to humans who had treated me so terrible.

The worst life I had that was difficult to overcome was with a wagon train moving across barren cold grounds, little food, sometimes no water, whipped continually as we had little strength to pull the wagons. Some held people. Some were so heavy-laden; I don't know with what. I was skinny, sickly. The worst of all brutally whipped.

There was a river to cross with fast-moving water. Fear was in all—men, women, and children. More than any was our fear, weak, not strong enough to not only stand up to the rushing waters but also to pull the wagons. Death for me was terrible as I did not pass right away. I was dashed against rocks, still with part of the wagon attached to me, holding me down under the water. I surfaced only to be carried down a rapid falls. Finally, I passed over, brutally battered, pain, broken bones, thankful this life was over.

With me, I took rage anger as the brutality of man, so ravaged was my body, my mind. I am sorry I could not respond to anything, just inner hate to all. I am trying again. I asked to return to you in an effort to show you love and respect. I still have pieces of me that may come to surface that I will try to overcome with your patience. Don't abandon me. I will try, but be careful of me until I am sure all bad things are gone.

Second Ebony, same, but nicely different, just for you.

Third Message from Ebony Describing His Life before His Current Home

You ask that I come to you in writing again. My beginning in this life cycle was of no consequence. Secure, looked after, nourished by a caring mare, I was raised to be sold, I think. No one really cared for me, just a horse to make money. This is what it seemed to me. I had no care as I didn't know what it meant. I was to be controlled quickly, trained to be sold.

The man was mean, no care, only rush to make money. He never whipped me but had a whip that he cracked. I was so scared I didn't know what to do, too scared to understand how or what I was to do. No kindness, just always threatened with that horrible snapping whip.

I seemed to remember I was to be an obedient, loved animal. This was not happening. I was panicking, wanted to return home. This man said he gave up with me. He didn't have the patience or time to spend on such an ignorant horse, so I was sold. A short time, and I was sold again. They didn't want to try to help me or even care. Just not worth the effort; didn't like me.

Old memories were coming back to me, so I didn't care that they couldn't train me. I craved to be wanted, a tender hand, but this was not for me. I became depressed. I felt encouraged to go on but didn't know why. Really lost. I don't know what scared means.

I do remember when I was young, still small, they wanted to brand me in order to know which herd I belonged to. I was in the third herd; others were different. I heard them talk. When it was time to sell, they would know which herd was those. Many horses, I think, for different purposes. When they did this to us, screams were all around us, the terror, pain never to be forgotten. I now have found the tender hands, maybe care and love to accept.

Ebony

Ebony explains why he chose to return to the same owner in this life cycle. In his past life cycle, Ebony was an unruly hard-to-handle mare. Unpredictable and dangerous, she was eventually sold by the owner. Ebony remained distrustful and hateful of humans until her passing. On the Other Side, she received the necessary healing to return to a new life and chose to redeem himself by returning to the same owner from her last life.

Since humans, like animals, have the gift of free will, there was a possibility that Ebony would not have been purchased by his previous owner. However, as fate would have it, the previous owner saw Ebony and was immediately drawn to him. Currently, Ebony is still fearful of humans but is slowly learning to trust.

Ebony and his new owner were starting to connect and trust one another. After approximately six months the owner began to commence with his training. While dismounting, Ebony got scared and ran over his owner. After this incident, Ebony would not let his owner near him. A writing was requested to establish the reason for his current distrust.

<u>Ebony's Message About His Fears</u>

This is the one still called Ebony.

Determined to become a horse like the others that I see. They are settled, happy, obedient, not upset and afraid like me. Anytime I hear a sharp crackle sound, I am back to a time of fear I could never overcome. The life before keeps coming back, like all around me. I seem more in that life than this one. They are not the same, but memories make me feel it will happen again.

I remember somewhere, someplace, I was afraid of men. I do not like them as they are always cruel; never has one been kind. They panic me. I am now afraid of everything, everyone, even her. I hurt her. She feels badly. She says she is hurt. She thought she had gained my trust. How can I trust anyone anymore if I can't trust myself? I am well looked after, so why should I not feel safe.

QUESTION: What can be done to make you trust yourself and her?

Ebony's REPLY: *Let me get used to what is around me. Know that I can feel secure, familiar so that the terrible times are not really here all around me. That man won't come in and hurt me. Punish me,* ride me, angry with me. They do things that hurt, then I can't eat, but it only makes me worse in pain. Could you let me come to you when I am ready to?

A Lost Ebony

Ebony's Fears Reinforced in the Life

I care for my lady. Never wanted to hurt her. When I passed over from before when I was so mean to her, I saw how horrible I was to her. She didn't deserve that, but I had been beaten, little food in that prior time. When I returned, I still had memories. I said if I could return, I would make up for it.

Since I came back to the life cycle, there has not been anyone I could trust. I endured cruelness again and again. Bitterness flooded me, changed me back to all the horrible memories I thought I had left behind so I could enter this life renewed. The last thing that was so terrible for me was the mean man, then another one worse. He put something cruel in my mouth. He was impatient. If I didn't understand what he wanted, he would jerk and pull until my mouth was all cut up. That night, it hurt so much I couldn't eat. I was hungry but just couldn't stand the pain. The next morning, he did the same thing. My mouth was bleeding, but he still jerked and pulled. I don't know what I did; I just wanted to get it out of my mouth. I would have taken a whipping rather than this. I don't want to be untrustworthy.

Lady says she does not know if she can trust me. I can't trust myself. I don't even know what happens to me. I think fear, scared. I think I need time to feel secure, know I won't be mistreated again, to be mean again.

When on the Other Side, I felt guilt as to how I acted. Now, determined to be good, obey, but I am not sure how to do this. I don't know what or how to behave. Maybe the other horses will help *me. I need help. I think if I can sort things out, I can become the horse I had planned to be when I was allowed another life cycle. I let myself down, returning to all the old fears and meanness. Shame for me. If I am given time, like when I was on the Other Side, it would help.*

First, trust within me, then win Lady over for her to trust me too. How can she be forgiving? Two life cycles with me. Lady's thoughts are so like her; she wants to keep me forever. This is what I want, too.

QUESTION: Are you ready to be trained?

Ebony's REPLY: *I am not sure what that is. I heard them talk that he would have me trained in no time. That was horrible. I don't know if I could stand the pain.*

STATEMENT: Lady will tell you training is your desire to please her and know commands. She will explain it to you.

QUESTION: Do you want someone nice and kind to train you away from Lady?

Ebony's REPLY: *No, no, please, no. I will behave, try really hard, no more, please. Training whatever it is, I would try for Lady. Do not hurt my mouth. Give me time to heal like on the Other Side. Lady, my Angel.*

Past lives can be a critical influencing factor on an animal's current mindset. In this case, Ebony entered this life feeling the mistrust of humans from previous abuse. The brutality he experienced in this life triggered these feelings, causing him to be fearful of humans. Labelled unpredictable he was discarded at different auctions.

When horses are sent to auction, sometimes it is due to changes in human circumstances. Some are old and deemed no longer useful, others have a physical limitation, while others are believed to be unmanageable or untrainable. Ebony was labelled as such a horse, an animal clearly misunderstood.

Most often, the communicator not only feels the horse's emotional state but may also feel its physical condition. In this case, the communicator could feel the blood and pain the horse was feeling in his mouth incurred by a severe bit and a bad hand.

Poco and Clair, Together Forever

Poco and Clair were both senior ponies owned by the same person for the duration of their life. Poco was rescued at three months of age, and Clair was a foal produced on the farm a few years later. Both were shown successfully by children and later were used in a children's camp. Now retired, they currently reside at another farm during the summer, where they are loved and spoiled. A writing was requested to find out more about these ponies.

Poco and Clair

Message from Poco, the Pinto Pony

You wish us to tell you our story. We are happy and content together; nothing to complain about. Extra, we are loved. This I will tell you both for me and Clair. We have had many lives together, some not so good but never mistreated. Our greatest heartbreak is if we are separated.

One life cycle, we were born twins. Clair died; I did not want to go on without my other one. I was cherished by children, the whole family. There was no want for me, only to be with my soulmate. I wanted to join her, tried to pass over, but I was too well looked after. In fact, I became very healthy. No hope there.

Clair told me I was selfish, only thinking of myself. She had brought enough heartache to the children and family by her passing; why would I add more? She was back home; I would join her when my time came. Shame on me for thinking I knew better than what our Creator had felt necessary. Learn to accept what was best for us. Remember this parting had been agreed to by us; know of the parting sorrow.

I gave in, enjoyed the kids, lived long enough to be there for the new offspring. The sorrow I had within taught me to love what I had, turn my sorrow into companionship of the family that loved me so much. We are together in this life. No sorrow, no complaints. Can love and be loved.

Poco, shy Clair

Animals can not only have a strong attachment to their humans but can develop this same affection towards another animal. In many cases, when an animal has experienced numerous life cycles with the same soul, it chooses to return with that same animal to complete another life cycle.

Fanci – Misunderstanding, Regret

Fanci was a quarter horse mare owned by her girl for eleven years. A show horse in her early years, then a broodmare, Fanci did it all. When Fanci started kicking the fence and the stall, it was thought that she had turned sour, never a thought that she had a physical condition. There was instant regret after selling the mare. The owner reached out decades later for a reading to see what had happened to her beloved mare.

Message from Fanci from the Other Side

This is Fanci. I was not supposed to have a long life. I would have been more happy to stay with you till I passed. Many things I did not understand. I wanted to please you; you, in return, were good to me. When I got sick, I couldn't tell you what was wrong with me; I didn't know. I had to lash out, but I didn't want to hurt you so I kicked other things. I was angry how I felt. I know they call it pain. It wouldn't leave me; I was in such hurt.

I would never hurt you, no matter how bad I felt. It was not your fault, as I couldn't tell you. I would have liked to pass over with you comforting me. This did upset me. I was led away from all I loved. What was wrong with me passed. I was able to be good again. How I wanted to return to you. It was good where I was but not like you—so special.

They said I was eating something that caused the pain in my stomach. They tried different things, looked after me. Something they gave me made my stomach ease little by little. They changed what I was given to eat. I heard them say it was worth all the vet bills as I was a beautiful, wonderful horse. They treated me special. I had a special time growing up, love understanding, together with you. You were not mean to me, but neither one of us had the least idea what was wrong with me. Know I had a foal, how I wanted you to see him.

You would have loved him so much. I saw you once, I called to you, but you didn't notice. I wanted you to know that I missed you. I wanted you to see my little stallion; I was so proud of him. They named him Spirit as that he was, full of energy, a real challenge.

I have passed over having lived a good life. You did no wrong. My path was to be with another one who also loved me. You taught me so much. It was all positive with you, have no regrets. What to be was! Lessons are to be learned by you, by me.

Have no heavy heart; I remember only love and care. I had to leave as I would only have gotten sicker. It had to be so. Always memories, so good.
Fanci

When animals are sold or given away from a home where they have been cared for and loved for an extended time, they feel confused, anxious, and often sad, not understanding why they were given up. The beautiful thing about animals is that when they pass, they have a higher understanding and are thankful for the love shown to them during their time with that owner.

In Fanci's case, her original owner felt guilty from the moment the horse was sold. Fanci's message to her owner was of love, compassion, and support for her decision. Fanci emphasized that it was meant to happen. Some call it fate, as it was time for another to enjoy the love the mare had to offer.

Dodo Daisy – A Cow's Story

All creatures, big and small, have feelings, different personalities and appreciation when love is shown to them. Once the writing was complete, Daisy wanted to hang out with the communicator telepathically and wouldn't move on until she had her spiritual pat. Truly the sweetest cow that appreciates and loves her current owners. This is Dodo Daisy's story.

Message from Daisy

Some things I know. I am not the smartest in the herd. Actually, they say I am useless; I don't produce milk. I heard that I had brain damage. I lived, but the other didn't. Gillen produced good cows for milking. He also produced a lot of children. All were loved. I was different, this I know. Slow, never reacted to a bell to bring other cows home. No need, I had no milk, no problems.

One of the younger boys had the obligation to look after me. They were too busy to go find me. Alan told me he loved me. We both had the same problems, not too bright. We enjoyed being together, especially in a field of daisies. He named me Dodo Daisy; he said it nice to me. We were out in the field. The other cows had headed back at the sound of the bell. We just stayed where we were, enjoying ourselves.

We did not know a fire broke out at the barn. It was quickly put out, but panic broke out.

None died of fire but the panic of it. Many were saved, but some suffered injuries I don't know how to explain. This was a great loss.

Dodo and Alan wandered home to find a terrible situation. This was the only time my owner was angry with me. He said why couldn't it have been me to die instead of the good ones. Maybe I agreed. I just wandered off so they could not find me.

The other cows and me were friends. I felt their loss as friends, but my owner lost some of his business. I wanted to go home (Other Side). I was upset. Gillen could not afford to feed me, a useless cow that couldn't produce. He couldn't bring himself to use me for meat. He just let me wander off.

I joined a herd of cows, was chased away when they realized I was useless. I kept wandering around, no home until now. I thought I had passed over as every animal was looked after. There seemed to be such care for all of us that were damaged one way or another. I would like to be called Daisy. Such good memories, but Dodo is alright as it comes from someone nice. I am grateful for my home. Daisy

AUTHORS BIOGRAPHIES

AUTHOR

Growing up her talent as an artist filled her spare time, graduating to oil painting becoming an Artist, a lifetime love. When she was young, she always enjoyed birds, canaries, budgies then turtles and fish. Graduating as a bookkeeper, she soon realized this was not a career she wished to follow. She then graduated from the National School of Dress Design. Organizing fashion shows, dress designing was inspirational and fun for her. Later she started her own business, establishing a lucrative Dixie Dairy, selling packaged foods. Sold it within a year, realizing it was not what she wanted. She then applied for a government position with Unemployment Insurance, retired after 30 years as a Programme Administrator. During this time, she did volunteer work and received her second level Reiki Certification.

With three animal loving daughters, there was never a dull moment. Colicky horses, search and rescue, some emergencies always demanding immediate attention. Usually her, in high heeled shoes tramping through swamps for evasive horses. She could write a book on that alone.

Her true enjoyment in her life has been her writings throughout the years. Connecting with spirit to help those who had lost loved ones. The greatest challenge came when she was asked to write for animals. This was her turning point for the most rewarding endeavour for her. Now, to share these writings with other has truly been a blessing.

COAUTHOR

For as long as Karen can remember she has always had a love for animals. Her first pet was a little rabbit called CC. She would spend hours with CC taking him for walks, brushing him, and telling him all her childhood secrets. When Karen was 6 years old her older sister introduced her to horses. Her sister would take Karen to various riding stables where she would ride the big horses. When she was 7 her mother traded for their first horse, a palomino gelding named Cherokee. Karen would ride Cherokee every opportunity she could get. When other kids were riding their bikes and playing in the park, Karen was out playing Cowboys and Indians with her horse. That was the start of her lifelong obsession with horses.

As Karen got older her passion for animals grew stronger, as did her curiosity for the supernatural. When she got married, her and her husband purchased a two-hundred-year-old farmhouse. It didn't take long before strange phenomena started to occur. Music and voices were heard daily during the nighttime hours. Spirit manifestations and strange noises were common. This only heightened her desire to learn more about the other side. Karen started to read every spiritual book she could get her hands on. She joined paranormal groups and travelled to different active locations. It didn't take long before she realized that it wasn't earthbound spirits she was interested in communicating with, but higher levels of vibrational energy and consciousness. At this point, Karen started to take courses in Reiki. Soon after that, she took courses in hypnotism and became a certified consulting hypnotist.

During this time the animals on the farm began to multiply. Goats, pigs, chickens and of course horses became part of her extended family. Karen took Herbalism practitioner courses and learned to make healing tinctures and teas as well as all natural lotions, soaps, and cosmetics. She ran her business 'Elementelle' for about 7 years selling her merchandise and spreading awareness of the toxicity of commercial products. She currently gardens all year round and produces plant base consumables used for medicinal purposes.

Recently retired after 30 years working in the technical field as a Database Administrator, she resides with her husband on a rural farm with eight horses, a cat and five dogs. Over the years her home has become a sanctuary to many unwanted dogs and horses, giving them a loving and respectful space, and a sense of belonging. Karen treasures the companionship and unconditional love that these animals bring to her life and continues to provide them with a safe and loving home.

When her mother announced that she was prompt to share

the writings from the animals in book form, Karen eagerly volunteered to participate in this endeavor. The messages received telepathically from the animals has shifted her mind set in a whole new direction and has helped her grow spiritually. No longer does she see an animal just as an animal, but a gift from God, to teach, guide and offer unconditional love through our human experience. The opportunity to share their stories in book form has been an incredible journey and a labor of love for Karen.

Made in the USA
Columbia, SC
24 June 2025